THE WOMEN
OF HOLY WEEK

Readings and Reflections

VERONICA HUGHES and DEBORAH LANDIS

Dedication

To Dick Landis, who welcomed these 24 women
into his country kitchen as we wrote their stories.
We know they are still there, watching out for him.

Cover design by Chad-Michael Simon

Introduction: "We Were There"

In reading the events of Holy Week, you have already met some of the women in this book. We know what they did on Good Friday and Easter morning. *But have you ever wondered what they did in the time between those days?*

Our intent was to imagine what women were thinking just after the events at the end of Jesus's human life. Some of the women have no formal history, and not all are described in Scripture. But all of them have a story. Each one knew Jesus in a special way. Each one made a difference, adding a detail that illuminates the meaning of his life on earth. And each one offers inspiration as she shares her deepest feelings and insights.

In the years that Jesus lived on earth, women's place was clearly defined – in the background. Men dominated as leaders of their families and as keepers of religious tradition. As the momentous events of that last week unfolded, men's lives were based on action and reaction. They acted their parts, whether that was praising on Palm Sunday, sharing Seder, or plotting his arrest and death. We know what they *did*, but almost nothing about what they *thought and felt*.

However, women are very much in touch with their feelings and still more articulate in naming them. So even as the episodes of Holy Week played out, the women surely must have shared their thoughts, memories, regrets, and dreams as they continued their ordinary lives.

In getting to know these women, we were careful not to set them on pedestals. We believe that they often perceived what men did not, but they were essentially, exquisitely human. They were not always perfect, but they were undoubtedly instrumental in giving birth to the strong, gentle community that Jesus intended. Their experiences as women and as witnesses allowed them to help others, then and today, to understand what Jesus was trying to teach us. Drawing on the strength that came from mere survival and subordination, they went on to change not only their own lives but others' as well.

As we became close to these women, we learned to love and respect them. No matter what hardships and spiritual challenges they faced, they survived. Even at the end, they did not abandon Jesus – for they knew, as men did not, that there are many things worse than dying.

Now, as you visit with each woman, consider how we are still connected. Although 2,000 years have passed, we are still sisters.

Veronica Hughes and Deborah Landis

Table of Contents

The Women

Notes about names:

For women who are named in traditional writings, we use the Hebrew form (except for the three women named *Mary* and *Martha*) – *Elisheva*, *Shulamit*, and *Yohanah*.

We have assigned names to women who appear, but are nameless, in traditional writings – *Talit*, *Rachael*, *Rafca*, *Ellori*, *Kitra*, and *Ruth*.

We use the real names of women whose names are not found in traditional writings but are known elsewhere – *Claudia*, *Perpetua*, *Photini*, *Veronica*, and *Cyborea*.

We have created names for women who aren't written about but surely existed – *Halima*, *Deenah*, *Shoshanna*, *Tovah*, *Edra*, and *Naomi*.

Prologue

It was a world of men.
But we were there.

The authors of the gospels wrote the story of Jesus through men's eyes.
But we saw him too.

In the holy books, they gave us few words to speak.
But we have much to say.

They cast us in roles of the weak, the lost, the ignorant.
But we were mothers, wives, friends, followers, witnesses.

All of us knew him in different ways.
But we all loved him in the same deep way.

Listen to our stories, for they may be your stories too.
And we were there.

Elisheva
Mother of the Baptist

Mary's kinswoman Elizabeth, whose Hebrew name is used here, was the mother of John the Baptist. In her steadfast love for Mary and her understanding of God's expectations, she stands for unwavering friendship and optimistic trust in God's plan.

When God gives you many years, you see many things change – good things, sad things. Like this house that I have lived in for so long – it's no longer mine. Ah, but this is a good thing! I gave it to a young couple in trade for their care of me, the widow Elisheva, until I die. They talk of having a child soon. Another good thing! They remind me of myself and Zacharias, long ago. And of other children – two little boys, very special ones, playing beneath my fig tree, growing to manhood, soon to do God's work.

And yes, I have heard the news from Jerusalem. On this sad day, I could mourn the deaths of each of those boys. But because my own end is surely near, I prefer to look at beginnings instead. And there were many wonders in the lives of these two young men.

It began on that day more than 30 years ago when Zacharias came home from the temple, wild-eyed and silent, very unlike my self-righteous but beloved husband. With excited gestures and a few scribbled words on paper, he told me that an angel had announced that I was pregnant! And I had been childless all these years.

"Of course, you silly man," I laughed. "That angel was me! I've been wanting to tell you that since we got married!" He shook his head fiercely. "Gabriel," he wrote.

"Oh, a *real* angel," I said, teasing him. "So why can't you talk?" He pointed to the angel's name again, then stamped his foot in frustration, dismissed me with a wave of his hand, and went outside.

But could this be true? A baby! So many years I had prayed for this, and now this time it could be happening. It had to be true! Gabriel had said so! I savored this revelation, joy filling my heart.

As the months went by and I became sure of this miracle, when I thought I could never be happier, an even more extraordinary day arrived. I was sitting under my fig tree, slicing vegetables for dinner. A caravan passed near my road, and a young woman with a small pack got off the back of a wagon. She looked at me and waved. It was Mary, my sister Anna's daughter, from Nazareth! As I watched her approach, I noticed something different about her. It had been only a few months since I had seen her last, but she looked more womanly, more feminine than I remembered. Was this the little girl who had run races with the village boys – and won? I only know that all the sunlight in the sky seemed to be radiating from her face.

Mary shouted, "Aunt Elisheva!" She dropped her pack and ran to me. We embraced, laughing and crying. I held her at arm's length and looked into her eyes.

And I knew. In that one moment, the baby inside me danced, and I knew that Mary's body held our Messiah. How, you ask? Call it divine inspiration. Women's intuition. Second sight. Or all of these! I tell you, I just *knew*. And looking back, it pleases me to know that my John's little dance was his first announcement of the Messiah.

I held her face in my hands and said, "Mary, you are so blessed! And who am I that the mother of my Lord should come to me?" Mary's face was a picture of joy and relief. "You are my Aunt Elisheva," she said, "and surely I have come to the right place!" Then she dropped to her knees and said the prayer that Hannah said generations ago, thanking God for the gift of her own son Samuel – "My soul magnifies the Lord and my spirit rejoices in God, my Savior."

I made tea and we talked until nightfall. Zacharias' angel had also visited Mary and told her not only about her special role in God's story, but about me too. She had made an excuse to Anna about wanting to visit her favorite aunt while she planned her wedding to Joseph – a very responsible carpenter, as I had heard.

But we both knew that what she really needed was a safe place to rest, to be still, to talk things through, to fortify herself against what would certainly be a scandal back in Nazareth. God had provided this respite for Mary, and thus for Jesus, to begin this amazing journey. After all, she was so young for all of this! She needed to get through the delicate first few weeks of her pregnancy and become strong in body and spirit before she told all this to Anna – and, worst of all, to Joseph – and before the rumors flew.

It seemed as if Mary's life was moving too fast, and mine not fast enough. Here in our home where she had spent happy times when her family traveled to Jerusalem, she knew she would be loved and accepted, even by her grumpy Uncle Zacharias, who loved her far more than he showed.

Zacharias had at first doubted Gabriel, as I knew Mary's parents and friends would probably doubt her. But while she stayed here, the two of us *purely believed* – that we were both with child, that we would bear sons, that their names would be Jesus and John, that they would be childhood friends, and that they were part of the mysterious plan of God. We also knew, but never spoke of it, that her son might have to die for us all. But not mine...not my son too. John's sacrifice would be another surprise for me, one that I cannot think about now.

Once, in a moment of uncertainty, Mary asked me, "Why did God not give this honor to an older, wiser woman? Why not *you*, Aunt Elisheva?" Without thinking, I said, "God knows, Mary." We looked at each other and laughed. Then I put my arm around her and said, "He has his reasons, my darling. You will be remembered forever as the mother of Jesus. And I will always be here for you. Always."

For three months, Mary and I shared those happy secrets. Imagine...we were the first two people in the world to know and believe, and we were humbly aware of the magnitude of this. We were two simple village women, and one of us was to be the mother of the Savior, and one the mother of the man who would prepare his way.

Mary stayed with me until John was born. Then she went back to Nazareth as she had come – the mother of God waving to me from the back of a wagon.

So on this day after the end, I think about how it all began. Mary and I watched John and Jesus grow up and leave home to do the difficult work of God. And now both of us are the mothers of martyrs.

I am not able go to her, as she once came to me. But I will sit under my fig tree and wait. She will come very soon, I think, and again we will embrace and I will call her blessed. And we will be strong for each other, and keep believing, and be witnesses for Jesus and John. I think that our sons would expect no less.

Reflections on Elisheva

1. Elisheva is one of those people who always finds the best in everything. Are you like Elisheva? Who have you known who was like her? What were some comparable traits that you or this other person shared with Elisheva?

2. When Mary comes to visit Elisheva, she knows she will be welcomed, loved, and accepted. If you needed such comfort, to whom would you go? What does this assurance of acceptance mean to you? If you have never experienced this feeling, imagine what it would feel like. What emotions does it evoke?

3. On the other hand, have you ever been in Elisheva's place, when someone ran to you for comfort? What did you do to help this person? If you have never experienced this, is it something you might aspire to? Could you be like Elisheva for one of your own friends?

4. Elisheva's faith allowed her to believe in Mary's miracle before Mary even said anything. Her faith was deeper than Joseph's or Mary's parents, who at first doubted her story. Has this ever happened to you? Have you ever said, "I will always be here for you," as Elisheva does? How did you feel?

5. Because she is a religious person, Elisheva knows the prophecies. She knows what may befall the Messiah. She may suspect what will happen to her own son, yet she is completely optimistic about the plans of God. What does this say about her? In her place, would you be as optimistic? Why or why not?

6. Mary repeats the prayer of Hannah from the Old Testament. Do you know this prayer? You may want to look up this passage and compare it to Mary's Magnificat. Which version do you prefer?

7. Mary and Elisheva are the first people on earth who know that Mary's baby was the son of God. Considering the traditional authority of men in that culture, why do you think God chose women as the first two to know? What message is in that choice?

8. Mary asks why Elisheva had not been chosen to be Jesus's mother. Have you ever asked "Why me?" even when the unexpected event was a good one? Did you later change your opinion? What happened that led you to accept the reality?

9. Imagine the scene that Elisheva refers to where she and Mary sit watching their two sons play. What do you think this conversation was like? Think of what they might have said to each other.

10. Now, picture the scene that Elisheva mentions at the end of the story. Mary has once again come to see her beloved aunt, and now both of their sons are dead. What do you think they may say to each other now? What would their longstanding emotional connection mean to each of them?

Talit
The Awakened

Talit, the daughter of a rich man, lost her life and regained it on the same day through a miracle. Only one so young and fortunate could see death in exactly the way that Jesus may have meant it. She stands for complete confidence in eternal life, simple faith, and cheerful resilience.

My mother is weeping. Last night, she told me that Jesus is dead, that the Romans had killed him in Jerusalem. But I am not weeping. And my mother, of all people, should know better. Jesus isn't dead. He is just asleep!

When I was born, my parents named me Shifra, but no one has called me anything but Talit since I was 12 – since the day of my miracle, nearly two years ago.

My father, Jairus, presides over the council of elders in our synagogue here in Capharnaum. Father is a good, devout man, and he is well respected for his compassion and good sense. He said that Jesus was an excellent preacher, and it must be true since Father has seen so many preachers. Jesus was sometimes a dinner guest in our home. As a pampered only child, I was allowed to stay up and listen on those nights. I think Jesus felt safe here with us.

So as it happened, Jesus was on his way here to preach when I got sick. I don't remember much…only that one minute I was fine and the next I was gravely ill. But my parents have told me this story over and over, so I know it by heart.

My mother quickly sent our servant Ezra to the synagogue for Father. By the time he got home, I was barely breathing. Mother was beside herself with worry, but Father knew what to do. He set off in search of Jesus. Even then, Jesus seemed always to be surrounded by masses of people, some listening, some just wanting to be near him. So when Father reached the crowd outside the city, he had to fight his way to Jesus.

"Rabbi," he said, "I beg you – come to my house. My daughter…she is very ill!"

"Jairus, my friend," said Jesus, "what do you want me to do?"

"Just touch her, Lord," my father said, falling to his knees. Jesus was about to speak again when Ezra appeared. He said, "Sir, it is too late. Your daughter has died."

Father got up slowly and turned away, but Jesus placed a hand on his shoulder. He said, "Be not afraid, Jairus. Only believe."

And together, they led this crowd through the gates of the city, gathering more people as they went. In our street, they could hear our neighbors mourning and weeping, the flutes and drums playing the solemn songs of death. Our house was packed with people. In the middle of all this sat my mother, wailing in grief, supported by her friends. When Jesus entered, he held up his hands, asking for silence.

"Be quiet, all of you," said Jesus. "The girl is not dead, but asleep."

Now, none of our neighbors would be rude to a rabbi, especially in my father's house, but there were more than a few mumbles and whispers of doubt. Jesus wanted no dark thoughts to enter my room, so he took only my parents and three of his disciples in with him.

And I? I remember this part well. I was floating peacefully above it all, looking down on the mourners, on my own pale body on my bed, and on Jesus. I could sense the energy change when he entered my room. When I had gone out my body, the room felt cold and empty. Now Jesus had brought life back in by allowing only those with deep faith and good intentions to come near me.

Prayers for the very sick had always involved chanting, incense, sacrifices, and all that. But Jesus used none of these. He simply sat beside my bed and laid his prayer shawl – his *talit* – over me. He touched my hand gently and said, "Come out from under the talit, little one."

And suddenly, I was no longer floating above. I was back in my body. I sat up, the talit falling away. I stood up and smiled. I hugged Jesus and said, "What happened?" He laughed and turned me around to face my astonished parents, saying, "Now, feed this child – she's hungry!"

My father and mother rushed to hold me. Unbelievably, Mother cried even more, and she ran into the outer room to tell everyone what had happened. Then the musicians broke into a very different tune, and the people shouted with happiness.

Father begged Jesus to stay and celebrate, but he said no, he wanted to go to the synagogue and pray. As he left our noisy house, he told everyone, "Please, I ask you to tell no one about this." He knew that the crowds would grow even bigger now that he had raised Jairus's daughter from the dead. But surely he could not have expected such a wonder to stay secret for long.

Jesus had seen my stillness through God's eyes – as just a sleep from which I would awaken. He was teaching us new ways. No ancient rituals. No shows. No death. Yes, today many are weeping, like Mother. But soon, I know, Jesus will awaken just as I did. Just as we all will.

The day of my miracle seems so long ago. I am almost old enough to be married now. When God gives me children, I will have this wonderful story to tell them. And every morning prayer and every lullaby will begin with these words: "Be not afraid. Only believe."

Reflections on Talit

1. Talit tells her story simply: She was ill, she died, and Jesus brought her back to life. But from her parents' point of view, it was far from simple. Imagine what her mother felt when Talit became sick so suddenly. In her place, what would you have done? Why?
2. What is the significance of Talit's status as the daughter of a rich and important man? Would things have been different if she had been a beggar's child? How?
3. Anyone presumed dead was considered "unclean," and therefore untouchable. Yet Jesus has no problem touching Talit. How does this translate in today's world? Who are today's "unclean" people? How does Jesus show us how to act with them?
4. Although Talit was physically dead and was healed, many people in Jesus's time and in our own are spiritually dead. What points in this story could be translated into raising someone from spiritual death?
5. Why does Jesus bring only three disciples "with no dark thoughts" into the room with him? How do negative feelings counteract good works?
6. If freedom from the burden of sin is most important, why does Jesus choose to bring back to life a young, probably sinless, girl? What impact did this have on the witnesses? Would a spiritual resurrection have had the same impact?
7. Talit's simple view of the story may seem a bit naïve. How might a theologian describe this scene? Would it have been more dramatic?
8. Talit contrasts the old ways of mourning with Jesus's simple acts. Why do we place such importance on rituals such as singing, music, candles, incense, and other "props" when Jesus himself used nothing like these?
9. If you had been one of the neighbors mourning in this house, how would you have felt about what happened? If you were one of the "mumblers," what might you have said before and after the miracle?
10. Clearly, Talit's story foreshadows Jesus's resurrection. In what ways were the events similar? How were they different?

Halima
The Cyrenian

Simon from Cyrenia, in Libya, helped Jesus carry his cross. Halima is his wife and a witness to the crucifixion. In supporting her husband as he supported Jesus, she stands for devotion, understanding, and accepting challenges.

Passover in Jerusalem! I had waited for this for so long...and now I wish we had never come.

I am Halima. My husband's name is Simon, and we are Jews from Cyrenia, in North Africa. We had brought our two sons all this way, and how excited we all were to see the great holy city! Although we had never been to Jerusalem, it felt like a homecoming.

But a simple trip to the market on the morning after Passover changed our lives forever. We had left our lodgings, dressed in our bright robes, but before we could cross the dusty street, a procession stopped us. I pulled my sons close to protect them from the crush of people. Some Roman soldiers were leading three men, all with heavy wooden crosses across their backs. One of the men had been beaten so badly that he could barely stand. "A crucifixion, Halima," said Simon. "The children should not see this."

As we turned away, the beaten man fell heavily to the ground, the cross pinning him down. A soldier kicked him, yelling at him to get up. But he was too badly injured, and he did not move. The soldiers said something to each other and scanned the crowd. "You!" one of them shouted. He was pointing directly at Simon. He grabbed my husband by the arm and said, "Help him. Pick up that cross. He's supposed to die on the hill, not here in the street!"

Simon protested, saying that he was a Jew and could not, would not take part in a Roman execution. But the soldiers laughed, misjudging him by his foreign robes. "Do it!" they commanded, pushing Simon toward the still figure on the ground. Simon looked at me and said, "Take the boys! Go!"

I was frightened, but I had no intention of leaving Simon. I rushed the boys back to our room, sternly warning them not to leave until I returned. I waited until most of the crowd had passed, and then I followed. Simon walked beside the condemned man, carrying more than half of the burden. Together they labored under the heavy cross, through the city and up the hill. At the top, the Romans shoved Simon away and began the triple crucifixions.

I made my way to Simon. His robes were dirty and torn. A woman came to us and offered him a jug of water. He drank deeply, leaning against me in exhaustion. I wanted to take him back to our room, but he needed rest, so we simply sat on the ground.

Now, no one moved except the soldiers. The noises were impossible to ignore – the sound of the hammer on nails, the thump of the crosses as they were set into the ground, the grunts and jeers of the soldiers. This crowd of Jews – *of Jews!* – shouted insults, most directed at the man in the middle. What had he done to deserve this from his own people?

13

I asked the woman with the jug of water who this man was. She told us that he said he was God's son, our Messiah, and that his father had sent him to die for our sins. I looked up at this man. A small group of women and one young man had moved to the spot directly before him.

Soon the crowd thinned, but Simon and I stayed on the hilltop. The man said something, very low, and then his head dropped to his chest. He was dead.

The air grew suddenly still, as if the earth itself was holding its breath. Then the sky turned dark, the wind blew fiercely, and thunder rumbled. "Simon!" I said, "What kind of man was this that even nature mourns his death?" Simon stood and pulled me up with him. "Halima," he said. "Is the Scripture fulfilled? Is this really God's son? Did I help to kill him?" He looked down at his robes. "I wear his blood, and he wears my sins!"

And then my Simon – my big, strong Simon – began to weep.

We started our slow walk down the hill. Several times we stopped to look back at the stark silhouette of the three crosses. "Was this truly God's son?" I asked myself over and over.

And now, this morning, my husband and sons are sleeping in this room on a street in a holy city that we shall never, ever return to. Last night, some of the women we saw on the hill brought bread and wine for our dinner, in gratitude for helping their Lord. *Our* Lord.

On the chair by the window I see Simon's robes, covered in the blood of the son of God. I pray now that the man who died yesterday will help me find the words to heal my husband. And to heal all of us.

Reflections on Halima

1. Halima is a stranger when she is caught up in the drama of Good Friday. How do you think she felt when she stepped from her room to see Jesus with his cross? Have you ever witnessed a tragedy in a strange city? How did you feel? As a mother, what feelings might Halima have had?

2. This crowd – some irate, some distraught, all noisy and agitated – was Halima's first view of the people of Jerusalem. How do you think this added to her emotions? Have you ever felt the negative energy of a mass of people? How did you feel?

3. Simon tells Halima to run for safety with her sons, but she doesn't obey him. Consider this wild scene – no place for women and children. What would you have done? Would you have taken the same risk, leaving your children alone in a strange town to join an angry mob to be close to someone you loved?

4. The Roman soldiers may have chosen Simon to help Jesus because he didn't look like the other Jews. In most cases, being different means being excluded. But Simon became a big part of this story. How might Simon have been the choice of Jesus, not the Romans? What is the lesson?

5. Do you think Simon and Halima were destined to be in the street at that moment? Do you think it was just coincidence that they were standing right where Jesus fell? Do you think they recognized their part in God's plan at the time? Or later?

6. As Halima followed the crowd, she must have witnessed the other events that occurred along the way. How do you think she reacted to his meeting with his mother or to his blessing of the women in the crowd? If she had spoken to these women, what might she have said?

7. Imagine the scene at the top of the hill when Simon wonders if he had been part of the killing of Jesus. If Simon were your husband, what could you say to help him cope with this question?

8. When the other women from the hill bring food to Halima's family, what might that conversation have been like?

9. When Halima and Simon got back home to Cyrenia, how do you think their lives changed? When their family and neighbors asked about their trip, what do you think they said? Do you think they told the whole story? What would you have done?

10. Tradition tells us that one of Halima's sons later traveled with St. Paul. How do you think this affected Halima, knowing what happened to Jesus? What do you think was the last thing she said to her son when he left home?

Rachael
The Widow

The gospel of Mark tells us of a widow who, despite her poverty, offered coins for the alms box at temple. She shows us that no gift is too small in God's eyes. She stands for self-reliance, abiding faith, charity, and acceptance.

I have known many days, but these last ones have been the saddest of all.

My days are like coins in the alms box at the temple, each one the same, as they are for all widows. Every morning, the ritual begins – arise, pray, buy bread at Aaron's bakery. Of course, there you get not only bread, but also news and gossip. I have no need for such nonsense! Then to the market, household chores, supper, and it's time for bed.

Not much of a life, you say. I agree! But I thank God for the generosity of my nephew, Silas. He is a good Jewish boy. At least he *was*. He was raised to study the Torah and keep the holy days, but not long ago he heard of this carpenter, Jesus, and his beliefs changed almost overnight. I listened to the stories of healings and preaching, but young people's faith can be easily swayed. Where my faith lies, I *know*. I need nothing new.

But then some of my friends told me that *their* children, too, had begun to believe in this Jesus, and said he was the son of God. My friend Rebecca had even gone to hear him speak. I thought she was a good Jew, too, but she admitted to me that she believed in him! I can tell you this – I was curious to see what she saw. Ah, but I'm old, and walking any distance is difficult, so I never heard him preach.

And then, one day, I saw him outside the temple. Rebecca said, "Rachael! Look, there is Jesus!" I turned to see a plain man in a travel-worn robe and dusty sandals. "Rather common-looking for a son of God, don't you think?" I asked Rebecca sourly. But she had already moved closer to him. I didn't stay.

The next week he was at temple again. I noticed him watching me as I put my two coins into the alms box. He said something to those around him, but I couldn't hear what it was. His friends nodded and smiled. What had he said? That I didn't give enough? That was all I had! My offering was a real *sacrifice* for me! How dare he think my gift wasn't important!

"What was *his* offering?" I grumbled to myself. "What was *his* sacrifice?" I walked home in a foul mood, wanting to hear no more of this Jesus of Nazareth.

Not two days later, I heard voices outside my house. I opened my door a bit and saw Jesus in the middle of a small crowd. Rebecca was there. I closed the door quickly. Now, I may be an old woman, but still I'm curious. So I stood next to the window where I could hear and not be seen.

Jesus talked of giving, of sacrificing...that for an offering to be truly acceptable to God, it must come from the heart. And then he told a story of an old woman he had seen putting two coins into the alms box at temple, and how that gift was more pleasing to God than the gold of a rich man. Those coins could have given the woman some comfort, he said, but she chose to give them away.

I shut my eyes against the tears that came. He was talking about me! He was using me as an example of charity, and here I had been thinking ill of him and his followers. But he had recognized my sacrifice. I listened from my hiding place. He had a message of hope. Though we struggled on this earth, he said, his father had a better place for us in heaven. As he spoke, I came to believe that he was truly God's son.

And yesterday, when I went to buy bread, I found out that Jesus had been arrested and was to be crucified. His death would be an offering, someone said – a *sacrifice*. I hurried from the shop, leaving my bread behind. When I got home, in the stillness of my room, I heard my own words echo: "What was his offering? What was his sacrifice?"

I have my answer. Now I know.

Reflections on Rachael

1. Rachael sees her life as a ritual, doing the same things over and over. Do you feel this way about your life? Do you know someone who does? What might people miss by looking at life this way?
2. Rachael has drawn a tight circle around herself, avoiding people, judging their behaviors. Why do you think she does this? What may have happened in her past to cause this? Do you know someone who acts this way?
3. In the beginning, Rachael says she is sure of what she believes, and sees no reason to change. Why do you think she is reluctant to change? What emotions are behind this?
4. When Rachael first sees Jesus, she isn't impressed. What was she expecting the "son of God" to look like? Why would his appearance affect her judgment of him? Do you do this? How is this "normal"?
5. Do you think that Rachael's self-reliance is a virtue in this story, or does it keep her from interacting with others? Can we have too much self-reliance?
6. Rachael silently criticizes her nephew and friend for straying from their old beliefs. But we can see that she still loves them. What kind of conflict would this have created in her mind? Have you ever felt like this? What happened, and how did you deal with it?
7. Have you ever sacrificed as Rachael does here? Have you ever given something that was not part of your "bounty," but something you would have used for your own welfare? What were the circumstances, and how did you feel about this?
8. Rachael makes up her mind that Jesus is finding fault with her without knowing exactly what he said. Has this ever happened to you? How did this scene match what others in Judea were thinking about Jesus?
9. Unlike the other women in this book, Rachael learns what Jesus taught from behind a closed door. Have you ever done this? Have you ever been afraid or unwilling to face something new, even though it intrigued you?
10. How does news of Jesus's death affect Rachael? How do you think she may act differently after this?

Mary of Bethany
One Who Listened

Mary, the sister of Martha and Lazarus, was the unconventional one who neglected "women's work" to listen to the stories and parables of Jesus. She stands for joy in the present, thankfulness, equality, and faith in God's plans.

Over the hills, I see the light of dawn, the gift of a new day. But I have learned that there are many kinds of light and many kinds of gifts.

I am Mary, from Bethany. My father was a merchant who often made journeys to foreign lands in search of special things to sell in the city. He always brought back small gifts for me and for my sister, Martha, and my brother, Lazarus. Each time father arrived home, I would sit spellbound, listening to him describe where he had been. And when his guests visited, I would curl up in a corner, unseen, to listen. Men in strange robes and turbans, sharing stories of faraway places and mysteries... how I longed to know all this and be part of it! But I was a girl, and women have their place.

Another man visited often – Jesus – and although his robes were not fancy, the stories he told were more fascinating than those of the traveling merchants. Once, when Jesus was at our house, all the men had settled around him as he spoke. Quietly, I slipped into the room and sat outside the circle, hoping that no one would notice. But someone did – *Martha*.

From the kitchen, she motioned insistently for me to come help her prepare food for the men. I shook my head. She scowled at me and gestured more forcefully. This time, Jesus and my father saw our little drama. Father said, "Mary, help your sister." But Jesus stopped him, and offered me the choice to stay or go. I chose to stay. His acceptance gave me the strength to ignore the grumblings of my sister and the disdain of some of the men who see women as dust, not sunlight.

Jesus began to speak again and I was transported, lost in his words. When he was done, I went to help Martha. She would not look at me. I said, "Martha, please understand me. I am not like you, content to accept the role placed on us by men."

I saw anger flash in her eyes. "It is *you* who do not know *me*," she said, pushing past me through the door to serve our guests. Perhaps she is right.

And now comes this dawn, after that dark Friday. I have much to think about. Jesus did so much for me.

He gave me three gifts.

The first gift was to allow me to witness his inner world for just a small piece of time. To sit at his feet and hear his words, not muffled through a door or told by someone else, but straight from his mouth. He gave me the joy of basking in the light of his wisdom.

The second gift – a miracle, restoring life to my brother Lazarus! Because Jesus understood our sorrow, he commanded the tomb to give up its hostage. He brought my brother from darkness to a new light.

And now this last, greatest gift – the gift of his own life.

Once I craved a man's world with learning and travel, but I see now that this pales beside the life I will have if I live what Jesus taught. Being a woman will not hinder me, for he welcomed everyone, and his message was for all people.

How can I repay these gifts? How can I share his light? Perhaps I can tell my story to women who are struggling to find meaning in their lives. They must know that they are beloved daughters of God, that they too can lead others to the ways of Jesus.

I believe that we can all be gifts. I believe that we can all be the light. I believe – because Jesus taught me how.

Reflections on Mary of Bethany

1. Mary appears as the "spoiled" daughter who is allowed special favors by a doting father. Do you know people like this? Were you like Mary? How did this shape your personality? What were the good points as well as the bad?
2. Given the same situation – a house full of fascinating strangers – Mary and Martha react in different ways. Which sister are you most like? How do both sisters serve in their own manner?
3. In a time when women were typically assigned lesser roles, Mary dreams of traveling "in a man's world." If you had been Mary's childhood friend, what might she have told you about her hopes and dreams? As a traditional child, what would you have said to her?
4. Imagine a scene in the kitchen of Mary's home on the day of a visit from travelers. What might the sisters have said to each other? What would have been the important points each would try to make?
5. Mary speaks of three gifts. Think about your life. What gifts have you been given?
6. Of Mary's gifts, one was a miracle. Have you witnessed a miracle – of any size? What made it a "miracle"? How did it change you?
7. Mary values shared time as a gift. Do you agree? When has someone given you the gift of time? How did you feel? When *you* have given the gift of time, how did it change you?
8. Mary decides that being a woman will not get in the way of living as Jesus lived. Would this have been difficult in her world? What might she have had to overcome to do this?
9. Mary decides to focus on helping women understand their part of God's plan. Would she have made the same decision if she had joined Martha in the kitchen? How does she come to this decision?
10. Mary concludes that "we can all be gifts." How are you a gift? Who is the greatest gift in your life? Why?

Claudia
The Roman

The gospel of Matthew tells us of the wife of Pontius Pilate, who dreamed of the innocence of Jesus and tried to save his life. As the only person to stand up for him at his trial, she represents justice and acceptance of God's will.

From my window, I can see all of Jerusalem. It is a world away from Rome. The streets are dirty, the houses are crude, and most of the inhabitants are both, I'm afraid. But I can see it all.

Yet, I can see so much farther. This Jew we killed yesterday...I saw him in my mind for three years. And now, whenever people remember his name, they will also remember the name of my husband – Pontius Pilate.

Despite what you may believe, my husband is not a cruel man, or one easily manipulated. But keeping the peace in a backwater post like Judea is not easy.

I grew up in other palaces. I am the Lady Claudia, granddaughter of the emperor Augustus Caesar. As a child, I witnessed treachery, political bargaining, even murder. Everyone, it seems, wants power. And here in Jerusalem, people are also willing to kill for power. Yes, I could have stayed in Rome while my husband was stationed abroad, but I came here because I love him so much. Now I am learning about a different kind of love in this unexpected, desolate place.

My knowledge of this Jesus began with the chatter of slaves. First, ordinary gossip, then talk of healings – even restoring life to the dead. A prophet who taught charity and goodness. A magic man who preaches love. Who would *not* be interested?

And then they said Jesus was the son of a god. Now, I know all about gods – Roman gods. They are jealous, demanding, and vindictive. So this man intrigued me, this man with gifts of words and mysteries who spoke of his father – a different kind of God – and of immortality, not just for gods and emperors, but for everyone. They said that this "messiah" showed compassion for strangers, lepers, and women – whatever their reputations.

So, for the past three years, I have been a sort of follower. Oh, I never saw the magic, never heard the speeches. But I could not put the stories out of my mind. And I wondered why this particular prophet should move me so.

Then, two nights ago, the night I had the dream, the streets were crowded with Jews, all wanting to spend the holy days in their sacred city. And in their midst, two factions collided – those who supported Jesus and those who meant him harm.

I don't know how they found him in that secluded garden, but soldiers brought Jesus here to the palace late in the evening. The religious leaders believed he was a danger and wanted him arrested. This was clearly a local problem, not a Roman one. So when they demanded that my husband dictate a death sentence, he told them, "This is not worth my time – take him to your own courts!" And he sent them to that pompous fool, Herod.

And sometime in the darkness of that night, I dreamed my dream.

I was in Rome, at the temple of the goddess Diana. I had brought a dove to sacrifice. I raised my knife, but could not bring down my hand. Then, the dove spoke. It said, "See into your heart, Claudia." And it rose up and flew away. Then I looked at the wall beneath Diana's statue. Illuminated by the candle flames, I saw four words written in blood: *Let This Man Live.*

I woke in terror but quickly fell into a deep sleep. I was wakened at dawn by shouts of Jews in the courtyard. They had returned with Jesus, still looking for someone to condemn him. I searched for my husband to tell him of my dream and what I believed it meant, but he was already out on the palace steps. I sent a slave to deliver my plea for the life of Jesus.

From this window, I watched my husband's face. He trusted my dream but he knew what Rome expected of him – to keep the peace at any cost. When he turned away, I knew what he would do.

As I told you, my husband is a good man, but even good men with power must sometimes get their hands dirty. His hands are beautiful and strong, but yesterday, he washed those hands in front of the crowd, forgiving his own sin but allowing the crowd to be the dictator this time. He had hoped that this Passover gift – the death of this innocent man – would calm a possible insurrection. But in pleasing the crowd, he may have caused a revolution.

And so I was a distant witness to the drama between Jesus, my husband, and that hellish crowd. From this window, I saw Jesus on the road, bearing his cross. I watched the crucifixion. I watched until the storm began. Then I hid in my chamber, very much alone.

And from this window, I see the people leaving the city this morning, returning to their villages after this festival and its many sacrifices. But my husband and I must stay. Every morning that we are here, I will look across the rooftops of Jerusalem and see that hill and those crosses. No matter where our duties take us, I will see that hill from every window.

Yesterday's rain has washed the blood from the streets. But it will remain on the hands of the men who arrested him, the men who crucified him – and the man who condemned him.

My own blood is royal, but if Jesus was the son of a god, then his blood was royal too. I will continue to follow him. We are bonded by our blood and by my strange, sad dream.

Reflections on Claudia

1. Claudia gave up a comfortable life in Rome to come to a hostile place with her husband. Her love and loyalty thus put her at the center of Christian focus on Good Friday. Do you think this was a coincidence, or was she acting her part in God's plan just as Pilate was?

2. Claudia was open to listening to stories about Jesus even though his acts and appearance were vastly different from those of the gods she was familiar with. How does this set her apart from some of the other women in this book? What can we learn from her openness?

3. In a world dominated by men, a woman's dream may have meant little. Consider the courage of Claudia in sharing her dream with her husband and then begging him to act on it. What might you have done in her place?

4. Claudia is the only person who speaks up in some way in defense of Jesus at his trial. Have you ever been in a position to be the only one to defend someone? What did you do? If you chose not to speak up, how did you reconcile this?

5. As a Gentile, it is even more surprising that Claudia tries to sway her husband's decision in favor of saving a Jew. In today's disconnected world, what would you do if you believed that a person of a radically different faith was being treated unfairly?

6. In Rome, Claudia had worshipped many gods. Though she may not have accepted Jesus's new teachings, she was willing to learn about them. How might the world be different if we all learned about other religions? How would it promote a sense of connection and unity despite differences in specific beliefs?

7. Claudia trusts her dreams and intuition. Do you think women have a special gift of "sight"? Do you have this sight? Do you trust it? Have you ever not trusted your intuition and later regretted it? Has there been a time in your life when intuition "saved" you?

8. For the rest of her life, Claudia had to live with the knowledge that she had tried and failed to make a difference. Have you ever failed in a similar way? Did you find the strength to forgive yourself? Are you reminded of the act by certain circumstances? If so, how do you deal with it?

9. Pilate is not a well-loved figure in Christian history. But he was following orders – peace at any price. He had to weigh the option of granting the mob its wish or following his wife's "intuition" and risking an uprising. What might Claudia have said to this man she loved so fiercely at the end of that day?

10. Unlike some of the other women, Claudia has no real friends to talk with about the events of this time. When she returned to Rome, do you think she shared her feelings with her family and friends there? What change might they have seen in her?

Rafca
The Bride

The joyous marriage feast at Cana is the first public miracle of Jesus. Rafca's wedding is the scene for this marvelous happening. She stands for joy, wonder, optimism, and gratitude.

The news arrived this morning. My servant heard it from a traveler coming from Jerusalem when he went to draw water at the well. The Romans have killed Jesus. He is gone!

So then...why am I not sad? Where does this feeling of hope come from? Maybe I feel this way because I know this: *Things are not always what they seem.*

You see, it's just over three years since my wedding. People here in Cana still speak it, of the wine especially. They say that none will ever surpass its glory. Never again will we taste such sweetness.

I am Rafca, and Jesus was a guest at my wedding. His mother, Mary, is a cousin of my own mother. They have been like sisters since childhood, and Mary brought Jesus and some of his friends with her. With the other guests, they enjoyed the food and the singing and dancing. We listened to the story-songs of Solomon and his loves, and tales of our ancestors. We didn't realize that Jesus was listening to other songs as well, songs the rest of us could not yet hear.

As I danced in my wedding veil and tinkling bangles, I was unaware of an incredible drama that was playing out in a corner of our tent. At that moment, only my servant knew about the miracle – and Eli kept that secret like the small bag of coins I know he hides under his sleeping mat. It would be a little while before we all knew.

As my wedding day ended, I began my new life. I became busy as a wife in my own home, and soon as a mother. But word always reached us of the gatherings where Jesus was to speak. So my little household was there on the day when Jesus told us all, "Blessed are the peacemakers, the poor in spirit, the meek." I sat on the hillside nursing my first son, Asher, named for his father's father. On the way home, we talked about the marvelous words Jesus had said. Unable to keep the secret any longer, Eli at last told me the story about my wedding wine.

As a servant, Eli was expected to be everywhere and also to be invisible. So on the day of my wedding, he was standing behind Mary and Jesus waiting to clear the table when it all began. Mary had noticed a look of concern on my mother's face. She asked, and learned that the wine was quickly running out. This would have been a terrible embarrassment to my father.

Mary turned to Jesus and smiled. She said simply, "They have no wine." With a twinkle in his eye, Jesus teased her. "Really?" he said. "And what am I supposed to do about that?" They looked deeply at each other for a moment. "It is time," the look said. Then Jesus leaned over and kissed his mother's cheek. Mary turned to Eli and said, "Do whatever my son tells you to do."

Jesus motioned to Eli to come closer, and he whispered, "Take those stone jars and fill them with water." Now, Eli knew that we had plenty of water in other jars behind the tent. What we needed was *wine*. Confused, he waited a moment for further instructions, but Jesus was already reaching for a plate of olives. Eli looked at Mary, who nodded. He thought it was a bit foolish, but something in his heart told him that this would be more than a mere act of drawing water.

When Eli and the other servants returned from the well with the filled jars, he reported back to Jesus. "What shall I do now, sir?" he asked. Jesus laughed and said, "Why, take a cup to your master!"

Eli froze in fright. Jesus was asking him to risk angering the host of the wedding! Jesus smiled at his reaction. "Just go do it!" he said. Eli obeyed. When my father took the cup and drank...well, you know how this story ends.

When Eli finished telling me all this, I could not move. The man who had just spoken on the hillside had done this for *me*. This man who had taught thousands how to change simple acts into blessings had changed water from the earth into wine from heaven – for *me!* Was I not the most fortunate bride of all time? If this was *my* miracle, I thought, what miracles would there be for those who deserved more?

I wanted to follow him everywhere as he preached around the countryside. But I am a mother and a wife, and I have duties. But I also had enough to sustain me. He had already given me so much.

And so two more years went by, and I never saw him again. But Eli did. I would wait impatiently for him to bring home Jesus's stories of love and peace, sweeter and more satisfying than my famous wedding wine. And today he is dead, they say.

But I will still learn from him. There is more to know, more to teach my two sons. See, they run and play as if the world had not just ended. Perhaps it has not. Perhaps it has just begun.

Come, boys, let's go home. Come along, Asher. Come along, Yeshua.

Reflections on Rafca

1. Rafca's story is as much about Mary as it is about her. Mary probably didn't plan to request a miracle when she left home that day. But she recognized the importance of the moment and had the courage to ask Jesus. Do you think she thought about such a moment as Jesus was growing up? What did this moment mean to her?

2. Mary says just four words that prompt Jesus's miracle: "They have no wine." Instead of asking for a specific action, she simply states the problem. How is this a model for our own prayers? How often do we give God "directions" instead of telling him our troubles and accepting his solutions?

3. Rafca's wedding wine is one of those special gifts that we don't discover until much later. Have you ever had such a gift? How did you feel when you realized what had happened?

4. Have you ever been given a gift that changed your life? How might your reaction have affected the giver as well as yourself?

5. Jesus's first public miracle took place at a family celebration. Most of the people who were there never realized that anything miraculous had happened. What meanings can we draw from this?

6. Do you think Jesus performed "private" miracles as he was growing up? What might these have been? What is the difference between a public and a private miracle?

7. In what ways do you think Rafca kept the story of Jesus alive? How do you think she told the story to her sons? Do you think she went beyond just family storytelling?

8. As Rafca starts her life as a wife and mother, she is no longer free to follow Jesus physically, yet she keeps close in spirit. Have you ever felt too swept up with daily tasks to "follow" in person? How have you coped with this? How might you do this differently?

9. Even when faced with the reality of Jesus's death, Rafca feels only hope. How does this represent her depth of faith? Is her simplicity a lack of understanding? Would you have expected a different reaction?

10. What kind of mother would you expect Rafca to be? How might her closeness with Mary factor into this? What qualities of motherhood in Mary might she have modeled?

Deenah
A Voice in the Crowd

We don't know their names, but Deenah represents all the strangers in the crowd who called for the death of Jesus. Caught up in doing what she believed to be right and then realizing her tragic mistake, she stands for self-knowledge and self-acceptance.

This morning, pretending it was a normal day, I left my home to go to the well. But somehow I found myself in the street instead, looking up at the hill we call Golgotha. The crosses from yesterday's horror are still in place. Why have they not taken them down? To mock me? To make me feel shame and guilt? To remind me that I killed an innocent man yesterday? Oh, not with my hands, but with my words. And they were as strong as the hammer that drove the nails.

My name is Deenah. It means "judgment." And though I did not know it at the time, I have judged cruelly.

It all began so simply. Some priests and elders asked my husband, Jonas, and me to go to the palace where Pilate would release a prisoner in honor of Passover. This is tradition. But this year, *two* men were to be offered – a thief named Barabbas and a man called Jesus. When Pilate asked the crowd who should be released, the elders said we should call for Barabbas.

So, yesterday morning, because we obey our religious leaders, Jonas and I made our way to the palace and joined the crowd in the courtyard. Pilate appeared with the two men and said, "To honor your holy day, we Romans will give you a gift! Whom shall I release to you? Barabbas, the thief, or Jesus, the preacher?"

I looked at both men. I knew neither one, but as I looked at them, I wondered if the priests had told us to call for the wrong man! Barabbas scowled, as if daring us to set him free. He didn't look like someone who was wrongly accused. Then there was this other man. Standing there with his head bowed, he seemed harmless and innocent. But if he was in Roman custody, and if the priests wanted him to be kept in prison, he must surely have done something worse than Barabbas.

The chant started with just one voice – "Give us Barabbas." Then others repeated the words. Before long, more voices joined and the demand built to a roar. As I had been told to do, I said the words too. "Give us Barabbas," I said, over and over, more loudly each time. People shook their fists and seemed to dance to the chant. Then Pilate held up his hand for silence. "So, you fools would have me release this criminal? Then you shall have your wish. But what should I do with this Jesus?"

I had not expected this question. I assumed that the quiet man would be returned to prison to finish his sentence. What was happening?

Somewhere in the crowd, a voice shouted, "Crucify him!" I looked at Jonas in shock. Crucifixion was the worst punishment Rome could give. What horrible thing had this man done? Seeing our confusion, a man near us said that Jesus had caused much trouble for Rome. "We don't want our lives to get even harder, do we?" he asked. "And he says he is the son of God! Rome will think he is leading a revolution. They will send more soldiers and give us more rules if this man lives. Crucify him!"

What he said was true. The Romans had made our lives unpleasant enough. This Jesus didn't *look* like a revolutionary, but if he could cause problems for us.... And so I joined my voice with the others. "Crucify him!" I shouted. Each time I said it, it was easier. And then Pilate raised his hand once again, and Jesus's fate was sealed.

Jesus was taken away, and the crowd scattered. Jonas went home, and I went to the market. But something – I can't explain what – drew me back to the street outside the palace as the soldiers were beginning the long walk up the hill with the three prisoners who were to be crucified. From nothing more than curiosity, I joined the mass of people who walked with them. I was horrified when I saw how badly Jesus had been beaten! Why had this happened? I still did not know his crime. Many people were shouting terrible words that I still could not believe came from the mouths of Jews.

By the time we got to the top of the hill, most of those who had demanded his death had gone away. Not many of us were left to watch. I had never been this close to a crucifixion before. I wanted to run, but I couldn't move. The brutality shocked and sickened me. I heard the men groan as they were bound to their crosses, the cries of agony when the crosses were stood upright. I saw the pain on their faces. I promised myself I would never again witness such cruelty.

It was then that I saw the sign above Jesus's head – *Jesus of Nazareth, King of the Jews.* What did that mean? Herod is our king, not this sad, dying man. What were the Romans trying to do? How could the elders allow this sign? Why did they not protest? Something was very wrong! All Jews know that our only real king will be our Messiah, when he comes. This pitiful man, hanging on this cross with only a few people weeping for him, was surely not our Messiah. And the son of God? What kind of God would allow mere humans to treat his son like this? What kind of God would let his son be murdered?

I had seen enough. As I walked back to the city, the sky grew darker and the wind became stronger. Something made me turn to look back at the hilltop. Just at that moment, lightning illuminated the middle cross, the one on which Jesus was dying. Terrified, I began to run, never looking back again.

Jonas met me at our door. "Where have you been?" he asked in a shaky voice. Hardly able to breathe, I said, "I went to the crucifixion. Oh, how I wish I had never left home this morning!" And I told him all that I had seen.

Long into the night, we held each other and wondered who this man had been, and why we had caused him to be crucified. I remembered that Jesus seemed almost resigned to his fate. He never said a hateful word to any who had hurt him. As others shouted insults, he was docile...as meek as a lamb.

No man could go through what he did, in the *way* he did, unless he had a perfect trust in God, I thought, *in the same way a son trusts a father.* And as those words came to me, I knew. I knew who he was, and I knew what I had done.

Out of blind obedience, I had failed to heed my inner voice, and I failed to recognize the truth until it was too late. And I – and all the others who were with me – must live with this and try, somehow, to forgive.

Reflections on Deenah

1. Deenah follows the orders of those in authority, but they misled her. How do you think she felt at the moment when she realized she had done wrong? Have you ever been misled by someone you trusted? What were your feelings?
2. If Deenah had spoken out to the crowd when she realized her mistake, what might have happened? How do you think the crowd would have reacted? What would you have done if you had been in the crowd and agreed with her?
3. Deenah joined the spirit of the crowd and became one of them for a while. Have you ever been caught up in a situation that you may not have been sure was correct – but you didn't want to seem like an outsider? How did you feel? What made you go on? Or stop?
4. Have you ever witnessed cruelty? How did you feel? What did you do?
5. It occurs to Deenah that Jesus didn't "look like a revolutionary." Would her story be different if Jesus had looked more like Barabbas?
6. Deenah is shocked at how the crowds turned on one of their own people. Have you ever been in a situation like this? Have you read about one? What were the underlying causes? What emotions did the event bring out?
7. Deenah is surprised by Jesus's response to those who mistreated him. How does this lead to her understanding of who Jesus was?
8. Trust is a theme at the end of this story. Do you trust your parents as much as Jesus trusted his father? Are you the kind of parent whose child would trust like this? What can parents do to instill this trust?
9. Some of the other women in this book always act virtuously. Deenah is more human. How would you compare her story to some of the others?
10. Deenah feels that she will have to forgive herself for her actions – and inactions. Has this happened to you? Has there been an event that you needed to forgive yourself for? What process did you follow to do this? How long did it take? What did you say to yourself to allow self-forgiveness?

Perpetua
Wife of a Fisherman

Perpetua was the wife of Peter, the apostle. As part of a busy fishing family and as a good Jewish wife, she is a representative of many women of her time. She came to know Jesus through her husband and later became an ambassador for early Christianity. She stands for fierce faith, compassion, and the willingness to change.

It is unbelievable. What has happened this week is simply unbelievable – and this whole story was about *belief,* wasn't it? It's Saturday morning, and at last I have some time to think.

I am Perpetua, Peter's wife, and I will tell you what is troubling me. Since Thursday night, I have been waiting for an overdue husband. Yes, Peter has made me worry more than once. After a good catch of fish, he and his friends would celebrate around a fire on the beach, coming home well past dinnertime, well past kissing his children good night, and well past my good temper.

But now, where is Peter? The other wives told me about the arrest Thursday night and how shamefully my husband acted in the hours before the crucifixion. So is he running? Hiding? Trying to forget – denying his own denial?

Oh, how I resented Jesus in the beginning! He took my dependable, no-nonsense husband and filled his head with visions that nothing could alter. He stole Peter from me more completely than a tempting young maiden could have done.

For a moment, put yourself in *my* place. One day, out of nowhere, Peter calmly announced that he was leaving to go with Jesus. No, he didn't know where. Or how long he would be gone. Or who else was going with him. Or how I was supposed to keep our family in one piece while he was gone.

"How can you *do* this?" I shouted. "Am I no longer good enough for you? How can you throw away your family? And for what? To follow a dreamer, a preacher?"

Peter stayed calm – and this is not normal for him. He let me rant. Then he spoke quietly, simply. "All I can say, Perpetua, is that he is from God," he said. "If you hear him, you will see why I must follow."

And of course, the good Jewish woman in me told him in no uncertain terms that this was blasphemous! I went on and on, but in the end, he left anyway. I was abandoned. I felt unloved, alone, afraid. But still *angry.*

Everyone knows that men don't leave wives for nothing. So when my neighbors whispered about our little scandal, the only ones who still talked to me were the wives of the other men Jesus had persuaded to leave. We were a sad sisterhood. But after a time, we accepted it. What was our choice?

I heard many stories about Jesus, how caring and compassionate he was, but I had seen no seen evidence of this myself. So one day, I went with the other wives to take food and clean clothing to our nomadic husbands. Jesus was to preach, and a crowd was gathering.

Someone pointed to Jesus, who was sitting on a rock with children all around him. He embraced each one, as Peter had once done to our own. But one little boy stood alone, not far from me. He didn't move, but any mother could tell that he longed to play with the others. "Blind and deaf," I heard someone say. "So sad for his parents. Their sins must have been great."

Jesus began talking about loving each other, how we must care for each other like family. I heard, but didn't listen. What did he care for *my* family?

Jesus smiled as he talked, his gaze moving from face to face. Then, he stopped speaking. He walked over to that solitary child. Getting down on his knees, he put his arms around the little boy and whispered something in his ear. Jesus placed his hands on the child's head. The little boy's eyes flew open, and he leaned in to whisper something back to Jesus. He nodded, and the boy ran to his parents. Jesus went back to his place on the rock and continued speaking.

So this is it, I thought. Here is a man who would stop the whole world for a child. He would make all these people wait while he healed a little stranger, making him no more a symbol of sin, but just a little boy like all the rest.

In that moment, I began to understand. My closed heart opened wide, and I knew what Peter knew. I picked up my basket and walked to my husband.

"I believe," I said. He laughed and kissed me. He led me to Jesus, and I told him how sorry I was for not believing. Jesus held my hands, cleansing my spirit of anger and pain.

And here we are, nearly three years later, and the apostle Jesus counted on the most has abandoned him. Worse, they say Peter denied even knowing him!

I cannot believe it. I *will* not believe it until I hear the story from his own lips. I will wait. Again.

But this time, Peter will need more than *my* forgiveness, for he has offended far more than a wife.

May God give us all strength.

Reflections on Perpetua

1. Perpetua knew the meaning of hard work. How do you think this prepared her for her role as the wife of Jesus's chief apostle?
2. Perpetua calls this "a story of belief." In the face of increasingly unbelievable events, how does she cope? What were some of the strengths that were required of her?
3. Perpetua is continually asked to give more – first as a fisherman's wife, then as an apostle's wife, and finally as perhaps the only friend Peter had left at the end of this story. Have you ever felt this way – that no matter how much you gave, someone always wanted more? How did you feel? How did you deal with this?
4. When Peter told Perpetua about his plans to follow Jesus, she saw his actions from just her own point of view. Do you think her initial reaction was normal? Would you have reacted differently?
5. Think of the emotions Perpetua expressed on the night Peter left her to be one of Jesus's inner circle. Have you ever had a similar experience? What were your feelings?
6. What might Perpetua have said to neighbors who shunned her after Peter left to follow Jesus? What might they be thinking, and how would this have affected her?
7. Perpetua is won over when Jesus heals a little boy. Given how people felt about disabilities in those days, and given that her own children were now somewhat fatherless, what do you think she was feeling when this happened?
8. When Perpetua relents and talks to Peter after the miracle, how do you think their relationship changed? Has a single event ever changed the way you loved someone? How did you feel?
9. Peter's denial was one strange act in a night of many strange acts. But Perpetua is willing to forego judgment until she hears the story from her husband. What strengths in her were needed that night? Have you had a similar experience? How did you react?
10. Perpetua is a model of a faithful friend. Do you know anyone like Perpetua? Are you like her in any ways? What parts of her would you like to emulate?

Martha
One Who Served

One of two sisters who often welcomed Jesus to their home, Martha focused on duty, on performing the tasks traditionally assigned to women. But in her quiet service, she stands for patience, trust, and the realization that we are all jewels in God's sight.

"Thy will be done." Those were the words he taught us to say when we pray. *Thy* will, not *my* will. *God's* plan, Martha, not *yours.* Easy to say, but so hard to live.

But what happened yesterday...can that really have been the will of God? How can I understand that? And after all that he suffered, why are my thoughts this morning all about *me?* I am the one who always looked after others! The world has surely turned upside down.

By now I should have been married, tending to my own children in my own home. Instead, I have run my father's house, placing everyone else before me, acting as a replacement mother to my sister and brother, Mary and Lazarus, and growing older in discontent and despair.

In providing for others first and ignoring my own needs, I have grown bitter. No one looks at me as I go to the market or do my daily work in the house. I have made myself invisible to my family, even to myself, and I thought this would go on forever. But now I realize that *he* is the only forever.

And so here I sit, remembering the last meal I helped to prepare in a room like this just two nights ago. Unlike yesterday's horror and violence, these are memories I can touch without fear or sorrow.

On that Passover night, with the other women, I served those thirteen men – Jesus and the others – and tended to our ageless customs. Then I closed the door of the supper room and sat alone...as usual. The other women chatted about their husbands and children, and I have neither. But I do *think*, although they never ask my opinions. I kept my mind on necessary tasks, listening only to the hum of the men's conversation from behind the door. And so I noticed when their talk abruptly stopped. Then, clearly, I heard Jesus speak about bread and wine, and how it was meant to remind them of his body and blood. I did not understand, but I will always remember the words he spoke.

It was then that I noticed a golden luster shimmering in the space beneath the door, curiously brighter and more real than the few candles should have offered. The light grew brighter, and – I may have imagined this, but it was so real to me – it seemed to glide toward me. Was this my own mystical gift from Jesus? I stretched my arm out to the light, and it moved through my hand into my body and into my soul. I sat transfixed, bathed inside and out with this holy light. I was wrapped in peace.

I lost track of time, my mind quiet and serene. Then, the door opened. Jesus passed me, his hand brushing mine to seal the light within me. The eleven men who followed him seemed like shadows. One said they were going to the garden to pray. The men seemed dazed, less with Passover wine than with questions that they could not yet form into words.

I didn't tell the other women about the light. This was my secret, and they may not have believed me anyway. So we went to our separate rooms, not realizing that we were only hours from the end.

And today, with my heart filled with so much pain and so much wonder, I know one thing for certain. I have a soul that is worth the world and more. I have a light within me that flames gently but powerfully. I am no longer invisible. And I know that this sadness is not forever. Taking comfort in the light he kindled in me, I will wait to do whatever he asks of me next.

I am good at waiting.

Reflections on Martha

1. Compared to her sister Mary, Martha is often overlooked or misjudged as someone who chose the wrong role. Do you agree?
2. Martha has been the "responsible" sister. How might this have shaped her personality and affected her actions? Have you ever been in such a position? Do you know someone like Martha?
3. Do you think Martha is justified in her feelings of resentment? After all, she *chose* to work behind the scenes. How does a sense of duty sometimes evoke jealousy?
4. Like many of the other women in this book, Martha has her own miracle. Why do you think Jesus waited until the end to give such a gift to Martha? Or do you think he had been giving her gifts all along?
5. Martha says a light was kindled within her on the night of the Last Supper. Do you think this is so, or could it have been there all along? Do we all have a light within us? Or do we need a special event to make it come to life?
6. Martha serves quietly, invisibly. How is her devotion and faith different from the women who had more active roles in Jesus's life? Is there a difference?
7. If Jesus had ever stepped into Martha's kitchen, what might he have said to her? How might she have reacted? Why?
8. If Martha had come out of her kitchen and sat with Mary to listen to Jesus, how might this have changed her? What would have been Mary's reaction?
9. Martha is a model for patience. What things about her life may have helped her to perfect this virtue? How may those same events have sparked an opposite reaction?
10. Martha says that she is good at waiting. In what ways are all women called on to wait? How do we react to this? When have you been patient about waiting? Impatient? How did you grow through both reactions?

Shoshanna
In Bethlehem

There was an inn at Bethlehem, there was an innkeeper, and there was an innkeeper's wife. Shoshanna had the good fortune to be in the right place at the right time. In helping a young woman in the act of bringing God into the world, she stands for unquestioning love, active charity, and sisterhood.

The stable looks exactly the same as it did on the night he was born. When I heard he was killed, I took my lantern and came down here to pray, to cry a little, and to remember.

You probably know some of this story – but not as well as I do. I am Shoshanna, wife of Nathan, keeper of the oldest inn in Bethlehem. Our sons run it now, but back then it was just Nathan and I.

I remember how busy it was that week. People traveled to their families' hometowns to obey the latest demand of the Romans – a counting of all the citizens. It was a foolish idea, for many of us have no real home, but it certainly brought us business – more than we could handle. By nightfall, all our rooms were filled. I went to bed exhausted, knowing how much work was waiting for me the next day.

Sometime during the night, I was awakened by a cry. The town was quiet now, so I heard it clearly. It came again. I jostled Nathan awake. "Did you hear that?" I said. "Someone is crying!" Nathan mumbled, "Oh yes...there is a young couple staying in the stable. We ran out of rooms." And he was asleep again in an instant. That is Nathan.

But now I was wide awake, so I grabbed a shawl, lit a lantern, and went behind our inn, here, to this stable. Now, stables being what they are, I smelled it before I saw it. Did you think it was clean? It's a *stable*, after all – just a hard dirt floor, moldy hay and straw, and farm animals.

I raised my lantern, and there in the corner lay a young girl, clearly ready to give birth. A man – her husband, I hoped – knelt over her, his face frozen in fear and confusion. "You need help," I said. No questions were required. I hung the lantern from a nail on a beam so at least they would have light, and hurried back to the inn. It wasn't hard to see the path, as the stars were very bright...one in particular...but I had no time for stargazing.

I had delivered babies before. Few women in a town the size of Bethlehem had not. So I gathered clean rags, twine, a knife, and a blanket and went back to the stable. I asked their names. Joseph told me, but he still did not move. Seeing that he would be but little help, I sent him to the well for water. It's best to get men out of the way when babies come.

Poor little Mary! She had the sweetest smile, and she apologized for waking me. I told her that crying out was all right – that all children make their mothers cry many times in their lives. I didn't know then, of course, how much her body and soul would have to bear in the next 30 years.

I settled her into a softer pile of hay and shooed the cows and sheep to the far side of the stable. I covered Mary with the blanket, and we waited. I held her hand and smoothed her hair, asking simple questions to keep her mind off the pain. They were from Nazareth, she said, where her husband had a carpentry shop. She had ridden a donkey most of the way. Dear God, I thought, nine months with child, bouncing all that way on a donkey. No wonder this baby wanted to be born!

Joseph came back with the water. He still looked terror-stricken. So I sent him back out again, this time for food – somewhere, anywhere. This was women's time. You didn't really think a *carpenter* delivered that baby, did you?

He came back just at the moment when, at my urging, Mary pushed that little boy out of her body. This time I sent Joseph out to brag. There were shepherds in the valley, and I could hear him shout to them, "He is born! He is born!"

So it was I who helped Mary move to a fresh pile of hay, cleaned things up, and wrapped her son tightly in the soft cloth she had brought just for this possibility. I kissed the baby and handed him to his mother. She told me that she would name him Jesus.

They stayed in our stable for some time. I don't remember exactly how long – days, weeks. Nathan offered them a room, but Mary and Joseph insisted that they were comfortable in the stable – that we had already done so much for them. One morning they were gone, without a word. But our stable was somehow different.

And so life went on. A few years ago, I heard of a man whom people called the Messiah, but until today, when more stories were told, I had never made the connection.

A carpenter…like Joseph.

From Nazareth…but born in Bethlehem.

About 30 years old…named Jesus.

And they crucified Him.

I remembered Mary's baby, the child I had kissed when he was just a few minutes old. I grieve that I never saw him again. Such a tale I could have told him, and what wondrous things he could have told me.

I will watch the sky for that star. Maybe it will come again. Maybe we will all have another chance to know him.

Reflections on Shoshanna

1. Although she hadn't thought about it for many years, Shoshanna recalls the night of Jesus's birth with perfect clarity. Have you ever had such an experience? What kinds of events would engrain themselves in your memory so permanently?

2. When she finds the young couple in the stable, Shoshanna simply says, "You need help." Do you know someone like Shoshanna, who can size up a situation and know what to do instinctively? How does this attitude affect the people who need help?

3. The concept of happenstance – being *where* you're needed *when* you're needed – is a big part of Shoshanna's story. Have you ever found yourself in a situation like that? What did you do? What might have happened if you had *not* acted?

4. We often think of Mary as one who comforts. But Shoshanna had the opportunity to comfort Mary during a frightening, painful time. Do you think this act of kindness changed Mary in some way? How do even strong people react to kindness like this?

5. Shoshanna tells us that she kisses the baby. She is one of the first to do this; Judas is one of the last. How do kisses figure in the life of Jesus?

6. Shoshanna interacts with two men in this story – Nathan and Joseph. What is her attitude toward each of them? How does this contrast with her attitude toward Mary?

7. Until this night, Shoshanna had not realized that the baby in the stable was the one called the Messiah. Do you think she would have acted differently on that first night had she known this?

8. Shoshanna says that when the little family left, the stable was "somehow different." What do you think she meant? Do you think we all leave places "somehow different"?

9. This story points out the effect of our actions on others even when we aren't aware of them. If Joseph and Mary had stayed in someone else's stable, their story would have been the same. But Shoshanna's life was changed because it was *her* stable. Has someone ever unknowingly helped you like Shoshanna helped Mary? Do you think that person came away changed? Do you think they ever realized that change?

10. Does the realism of the night Shoshanna describes differ from the way you envisioned the first Christmas? Do you think it's closer to the truth, or is it too ordinary?

Ellori
The Healed

The lepers had no names; to name them would be to accept them. Ellori is one of these, but in her darkest moments, Jesus brings a miracle to her. She is not the one who thanked him then, but as one who does not forget, she stands for gratitude and trust in God's forgiveness.

The sky is changing color. It will soon be dawn. My husband and children are still asleep, and I am alone with my thoughts. They trouble me. I try to sort out my emotions as Daniel, my fisherman husband, sorts his catch on the shore, but I cannot. Sadness spills into gratitude, and fear spills into regret. And over it all, the wondering of what life would have been like without Jesus. And I go back....

The leprosy started as a small spot on my arm, and when it spread, I was forced to leave my family. My children were just three and four, and their cries echoed in my mind, tormenting me on my journey to the caves outside the city walls. My husband and mother promised they would not let the children forget me.

Every day I saw my future in the faces and hands of the others around me. In this place of despair, spirits were broken as well as bodies. We were empty, hopeless souls in exile. My body ached, not from the disease but in longing to hold my children, to kiss my husband. Memories haunted my nights and clouded my days. I was dying a little piece at a time.

And then one day, it was my turn to go to the village to beg for alms. The ten of us could not enter, but were permitted to sit a little apart from the road, ring the warning bells we were obliged to carry, and call out for coins. People passed. Most paid no attention. Then my friend Miriam called out, "Look, Ellori! There is Jesus – the healer!" Others in our group called out, "Master, have mercy!"

Jesus stopped and looked our way. He didn't move, and my heart grew cold. Even a holy man wouldn't come near people like us. But he closed his eyes, raised his hand in a blessing, and said simply, "Go and show yourselves to the priests." The priests, you see, were the ones who had the power to allow us to return home – if we were truly healed.

I stood very still. I could not take my eyes off Jesus, watching him until he was lost in the village crowds. Only then did I become conscious of the exclamations of those around me. "Ellori, look at me!" someone cried. "I am well! And *you* are well!" I searched for Miriam, but I couldn't find her. I thought she must have already run ahead to seek the priests. As I hurried with the others, my mind overflowed with thoughts of home! My husband, my mother, and my beloved children would soon surround me. I felt total joy!

That evening, lying in my own bed with my family near me, I remembered – I had not thanked Jesus! It would have taken only a few moments to turn around and offer my gratitude. But I was so excited to be coming back to real life. After the priests approved me, I had run home. Tomorrow, I thought, I will find Jesus and fall at his feet in grateful praise.

But my tomorrows got lost, first in celebration and then in the day-to-day business of living. The only difference in my life was that I was more aware of the needy around me – and, of course, the lepers in the caves. I repaid my miracle by tending to these forgotten ones, but I had never given Jesus a simple "thank you."

Then, yesterday, I heard that he had been arrested and was to be crucified. I felt my heart pound. I had to thank him! Was I too late?

I left my children with my mother and ran to the street. Usually only a few people came to watch condemned prisoners being led to the hill. But soon I was caught up in a huge crush of people jostling for a place to see this man pass by. The dust nearly choked me, and the noise washed over me in loud, wailing waves.

Fighting my way to the front, I saw soldiers clearing a path. In the midst of this throng I saw the bloody, beaten face of the man who had given me back my life. I cried out, "Thank you for healing me! Thank you!" I shouted this over and over, as the crowd surged around me. I was pushed and pulled and finally thrown to the ground in the middle of the road.

I felt something sticky on my hands. The stones in the street had cut me, and I was bleeding. But was it just *my* blood, or was it mixed with the blood of my healer? After a stunned moment, I got up and followed this death march.

When I reached Golgotha, I was far back in the crowd. I could not see what was happening until the first two crosses were pulled upright. When the third was raised, the shouts grew louder. Above it all, I heard commands of soldiers ordering us all to go home – the show was over. People began to wander back to the city.

Just then, everything grew very still – the quiet was something you could feel on your face, your hands. The sky began to darken although it wasn't yet evening. The wind rose suddenly and whipped at my robes, but I stayed. I walked as close to his cross as the guards would let me, and I fell on my knees, still saying, "Thank you." I repeated my thanks over and over like a prayer. I don't know if he heard me, but I stayed until his family lifted his body down from the cross and took him away.

I was alone on the hill. The darkness and wind grew more intense. I wrapped my robes tightly around me and turned to go. Then, a voice... or was it the wind? I felt that some message was being sent to me. I prayed that it was the voice of God who said, "He heard you, my daughter. Be at peace."

I walked home slowly, thinking of that voice. It was time to let go of the guilt and embrace the peace. When I reached my house, I kissed my children, my mother, and my husband, hoping to pass that peace to them.

And, today, I hope you feel it too, because that message was for all of us.

Reflections on Ellori

1. Ellori was a young mother when she discovered her illness. What do you think she was feeling when she realized what this would mean? What kinds of emotions would she have experienced as she left her children to go to the leper colony?

2. As she spends time with the lepers, she said she was "dying a little piece at a time." Have you ever felt this way, either physically or emotionally? What kept you going?

3. When Ellori and the others saw Jesus on the road, they begged for mercy. Jesus healed them without saying much and without touching them. How much of this healing came from himself, and how much came from the lepers? Do you think we can heal ourselves with the help of God? Why or why not?

4. Ellori returns home and begins her life again, planning someday to thank Jesus, but time slips by and she doesn't do this. Have you ever neglected to express your feelings to someone until it was too late? How might the words have changed things? Would things have been different if you had spoken up in the moment rather than waiting?

5. When Ellori thinks she may have missed her chance to thank Jesus, she acts desperately, running after him and staying on the hill as long as she could. Was this necessary? Do you think God already knew of her gratitude?

6. As Ellori falls in the road, she wonders if her blood and Jesus's blood were mixed. What might this mean?

7. If Ellori's gratitude was sincere, she may have vowed to do more as a way of returning the gift. In what ways might she have continued thanking God for her gift?

8. Each of us has been healed by God in one way or another. Does the size of the gift equal the depth of gratitude? Is it harder to recognize a small gift? Is the gratitude any less sincere?

9. Think of a time when you should have acted but didn't. How did you feel? Did you eventually justify your inaction? Do you think it made a difference to the giver? Did it make a difference to you?

10. As Ellori's story concludes, she realizes that she needs to let go of her guilt and "embrace the peace." What kind of faith and strength would it take to stop blaming herself? Do you do this for yourself? How do you "embrace the peace"?

Kitra
In the Courtyard of Caiaphas

The gospels tell the story of a servant girl who offers Peter the chance to defend Jesus. Kitra may be young and not a part of Jesus's circle, but she knows what is right. As a witness to the lowest point in a great man's life, she stands for loyalty and speaking truth.

Did you hear that? Somewhere in this city, a rooster crowed. It's not an unusual sound at dawn. But the last time I heard it – in the first hours of Friday morning – *that* was unusual.

I am Kitra. My brother and I work here, in the household of Caiaphas, the high priest. I am a house servant and Hayim is a guard. We are not here by choice. Our father owed a debt to Caiaphas, and we were the payment. He gave us up easily, and then disappeared. We learned early about disloyalty, you see.

Let me tell you what happened. I had been upstairs when I saw men coming across the valley carrying torches and lanterns. Then I heard shouting as they approached our gate. I went down to see what the commotion was all about.

It's cold and dark in the open courtyard at night. The only light came from a warming fire at the center. I heard more shouting, then the gatekeeper swung open the big wooden door and those men entered. As they stepped inside, I saw by the torchlight that it was a group of our guards, and that Hayim was with them.

And then I saw Jesus. His hands were bound and a guard on either side gripped his arms, but he stood straight and seemed oddly unafraid.

I had seen this man twice before last night. I was near the city gates on Sunday when he and his followers arrived. It was quite a parade – people waving palms and chanting praises. And later, I witnessed the chaos in the temple yard when Jesus ruined the vendors' booths and sent everyone away. And I had heard of Jesus from others in Jerusalem and from gossip in our household. Miracles, healings, they said, but all I knew for certain was that people made a great fuss whenever he was around.

Both times when I had seen Jesus, I noticed a big man near him who seemed to be his protector. I had remembered the big man because he reminded me of my father. And this man was with Jesus when he came into the courtyard last night.

They took Jesus inside to see Caiaphas, but the big man was not allowed to go in. He went to the benches by the fireside to wait. It is our custom to serve all guests who visit our household. But it was late and there was no more supper, so I brought a cup of water to him. He was startled to see me, but he thanked me and took the cup.

When he gave it back, I said, "Sir, are you not one of Jesus's people?"

The answer came almost instantly. "No!" he said. "No, I am not."

I asked again. "But didn't you just come in here with him?"

His voice grew louder as he said, "I told you *no!* I don't even *know* him!" Then the big man strode away to stand near the gate.

I went back inside then to finish my chores. It was natural enough that this man would not admit that he was a friend of Jesus, who was clearly in trouble with Caiaphas. But I knew what I had seen.

When I returned to the courtyard later, the man was once again sitting near the fireside. "Sir," I said, "I'm sure I've seen you with Jesus before. You even have the same accent."

He stood up. He loomed over me and shouted, "Woman, I told you *I am not with him.* I don't know him at all!" And with that, he rushed to the gate and demanded to be let out. But the guard had orders, and refused to open it.

It was then that I heard the rooster. It occurred to me that it wasn't yet dawn. Perhaps the man's shouts had awakened it.

And then the palace door opened, and as the guards led Jesus out, I saw something I had not noticed before. Jesus seemed luminous, shining in the dark courtyard. And then the big man at the gate turned around. Jesus looked at him, a look filled with reassuring love and loyalty that the man did not deserve. The big man simply looked away, but I swear there was pain on his face. And then everyone was gone.

Hayim came out and we sat on the bench by the fire, and he told me what had happened in the olive garden, and why there was blood on his robe beneath his ear. "He is divine, Kitra," he said. "He is truly the son of God."

And this morning, in the courtyard, I think about what they did to Jesus yesterday, and what the big man said. And I remember how my father denied my brother and me, but we are still able to love.

Watching Jesus showed me how perfect love can drive out fear.

Standing in the presence of that perfect love, if only for a moment, will be enough to keep me fearless forever.

Reflections on Kitra

1. When Kitra questions Peter, she speaks the truth. What is the significance of the sharp contrast with Peter's response?
2. Kitra gives Peter a unique chance to prove his discipleship and loyalty. He fails. Have you ever failed to stand up for a person or a belief in the face of direct, truthful questioning? How did you react? How did you feel about your response?
3. Kitra identifies Peter when he can't even identify himself. Have you ever been in a position where you couldn't describe your own personal "identity"? Has anyone helped you see the "real you"?
4. Peter betrays his loyalty to Jesus in a different way from Judas. Was each man ultimately doing God's will? What do their subsequent actions tell us about them? Why were their reactions different?
5. Kitra is the first person to call for truth-telling about Jesus in his last hours. How does she set the stage for the other women in the upcoming hours of Jesus's life? What other examples of truth-tellers do we find at this time?
6. Kitra had seen Peter near Jesus before, so she knew the answer to her question when she asked Peter if he was close to Jesus. What do you think she felt when he denied knowing his friend?
7. Why do you think Kitra asked Peter her question more than once? Why was it important to her to get a truthful answer? Have you ever had to probe for the truth like this? Why did you do it?
8. Peter felt threatened when asked to tell the truth. Have you ever stayed silent when you had a chance to tell the truth? How did you feel? How did the experience change you?
9. Jesus knew that Peter had to survive in order to be "the rock" of his new church. Do you think Peter thought about this when he chose to deny Jesus? When Peter and Jesus looked at each other in that courtyard, what words do you think their looks conveyed?
10. Kitra says, "Perfect love can drive out fear." What does this mean to you?

Tovah
The Basket Weaver

All four gospels tell the story of a little boy who gives the apostles some fish and loaves of bread that feed thousands. Tovah is the mother who packed that boy's lunch basket. She stands for belief, the ability to change, and the value of giving.

My name is Tovah, and I have two loves. One is my son, Levi. The other is Jesus – the teacher who was crucified yesterday. This basket on my table reminds me of both of them. Levi is 8, and he has some rough edges, but a good heart. I came to love Jesus because of Levi's generosity – and because of this basket.

On a day like this one, my friend Devorah stopped by to tell me that she was going to hear Jesus speak the next day, and that I must come too. I had heard of Jesus – he was something of a local celebrity even then – but I had never seen him. So I said I would go.

Early the next morning, I baked some small loaves of bread. It's only Levi and me, so we don't need much. I put them in an old basket, one that I made when I was learning to weave. I was just a child, and I was so proud of my work that I scrawled my name on the bottom. And now, because another child – my Levi – seemed to be always hungry, I packed that bread to take with us. Soon, Devorah called outside my window and we set off with our children for the hills where Jesus was to speak. On a whim, I stopped at a vendor's stall and bought a few little dried fishes as a treat for Levi. I tucked these under the napkin in my basket.

There were so many people on the hillside! It looked like thousands to me. It took a long time to settle everyone down. We were lucky to find a place just at the base of the hill where Jesus stood. Then he began to teach. All time stopped for us. No one moved. What he told us spoke to our hearts as well as our minds.

The hours went by quickly and soon it was well past noon. I heard some of Jesus's disciples arguing about whether to send us home because it was getting late, and we all had a long way to walk. I heard Jesus say, "See if there is any food." One of his men asked the crowd, but no one responded. I said to Devorah, "Well, at least we were smart enough to bring our own food! *We* won't go hungry." And I reached for the basket. It was gone! I looked up to see Levi scampering up the hill with my basket. I was irritated, but also proud. The silly, sweet boy – how would that small bit of food help to feed a crowd this large?

But in a few minutes, the men began moving through the crowd. When they came to our group, there was Levi with them – carrying *my basket!* The men gave everyone part of a loaf and a fish. But I had brought so little! "Where did it all come from?" I asked Levi. Grinning playfully, he said, "Jesus just blessed it."

Devorah and I watched in amazement as the men passed through all those people, giving out bread and little fishes. And do you know, when they were done, they still had food left over! When everyone had eaten, Jesus told more stories and lessons, and then he wished us all peace and sent us home. When Levi came back to me with the basket, I found enough inside to feed us for several days. All the way home, we talked about this miracle. We had learned so much that day.

And last night, as the news arrived of Jesus's death, I sat at my table and looked at my basket. Absently, I turned it over. Above my scribbled black name, I swear I saw a golden cross. Another miracle. I wept with gratitude for this gift from a man who must surely be the son of God.

I will never forget the lessons I learned on the hillside. That when we give, we get back far more. That when we offer ourselves in a smile, a song, a silent blessing, we can multiply our own gifts. That if we don't eat, we won't make it home, but if we take in what God gives us, we will always find our way.

And I weep again, not in mourning for his death, but in gratitude for his life, for that miracle day, for Levi...and for my basket.

Reflections on Tovah

1. Levi's mother is not mentioned in the gospels, but surely she existed. In what other gospel stories might we imagine "behind the scenes" people?

2. What kind of mother do you imagine Tovah to be? How do you think she instilled Levi's sense of generosity? How do we teach our children virtues?

3. What do you think Tovah felt when she saw Levi walking with the apostles, distributing the fish and bread? What do you think her friend Devorah said to her?

4. As in other stories, we wonder whether God chose the players in advance. Tovah is a single mother – she never mentions Levi's father. Do you think this made a difference to Jesus? To those in the crowd who knew her? What is the message here?

5. How did Tovah change on the day of the miracle? What was her feeling about Jesus before it happened? How does this compare with her feelings on the walk home?

6. What would an event like this mean to Levi? What story do you think he told his friends about what happened? How might he have told this story to his children?

7. As Tovah grew older, she probably continued to make baskets. Do you think she changed her technique? Do you think she thought more about the interweaving of lives as she wove the rushes? What message would her baskets hold?

8. How do you think Tovah translated that miracle into a lifetime of believing and giving?

9. Tovah's story is about gifts. She believes that gifts we give never go unreturned. Have you ever given a gift and then received a greater one in return? Was it tangible or spiritual? Was it physical or emotional? What was your reaction?

10. After giving becomes a habit, we realize that giving is a gift in itself. Consider how people donate clothes and money to the poor. What happens to these gifts? Do you think the recipients send back a gift in return? What is the value of that returned "gift"?

Photini
The Woman at the Well

Photini represents several "outsider" groups whom Jesus touched – non-Jews, foreigners, those judged as sinners, and of course, women. She stands for intelligence, self-acceptance, equality, and good humor.

This is *my* well.

They call it Jacob's, but everyone knows it is mine. For centuries, women have come here for cool water and fresh gossip. These smooth black stones have felt the touch of many hands and have heard many disgraceful and fascinating stories. The yellow dirt around it knows footprints that trace the sad little history of Samaria.

Yes, many have claimed this well but, of course, it will always be mine. That is because I am Photini, the one they call the town harlot. So no one from my village comes by while I sit here. Those self-righteous busybodies would rather go thirsty than speak to me. I come in the heat of noon, while everyone else is indoors. Just as they come here at morning and evening so they can see and be seen, I choose noon as my own guarantee of solitude.

And if I want, I can charge strangers for the use of my ladle and cup. Of course, not many come by because this is Samaria. They say we are half-breeds and traitors, leavings of the hated Assyrians who conquered us. So, naturally, Samaria is a place to be avoided. Do you know that Jews who travel north from Jerusalem go 40 miles out of their way just so their feet will not be fouled by our dirt? I don't miss them at all.

But you may be interested in the story I have to tell. A story of how I once gave this water for free and got my own freedom in return. A story of a man who was kind to me – and I am not used to kindness. The ignorant ones say that my bad fortune is my own fault, that I am "evil" because five men have married and discarded me. Let them talk. I need their approval less than I need those five foolish men! So if you wish, stay and listen. If you don't, it is no great matter to me.

My story starts on a day like any other when I went to the well, except there was a stranger waiting there, gazing into the water. A Jew, I thought, from the look of him. I set my jar down, wondering how much money there was to be made here. I dangled my ladle impishly. He smiled and asked me to draw a cup of water for him. I thought for a moment, considering his motives, but I did as he asked.

I said, "Since when do Jews ask Samaritans to draw water for them?" He laughed and told me that he was a Nazarean – and everyone knows that nothing good comes from Nazareth either. He said he had come through Samaria on his way home from the holy city. His name was Jesus.

So we talked, the stranger and I. He knew about my past. This did not surprise me, because any loose-tongued Samaritan could have told him that. But he didn't seem to care. We began to speak of God, of all things. Now this *did* surprise me. Men don't discuss God with their own *mothers*, let alone women with, shall we say, complicated lives. This man treated me as if I had a mind and a right to use it.

I said, "You know, when the Messiah comes, what has happened to me will not matter at all. The Messiah will judge only my heart."

He smiled and nodded, saying, "Yes, I do know that." Boldly, I asked why. "Because I am he," he said.

These four little words stopped me cold. Now, I know lies when they come from men's mouths, and that is precisely why I knew at once that this was the *truth*. I believed him. I smiled back. We had a secret, he and I, and we talked of God until the sun began to set. It pleased me to think of those silly people looking out of their windows, shaking their heads, and sneering, "Another man?" My answer to them would have been, "And one unlike any *you* will ever meet!"

I thought how odd it was that this man had refused to follow that well-worn, wandering trail blazed by fear and hate. He made his own road, one that led directly – and, I believe, intentionally – to me. And why did he come? To tell *me,* of all people, just who he was.

I offered him supper, but he said no, he had to move on. It would not have looked right anyway, I suppose. When he left, I felt clean for the first time in my life, and I knew that I would always be thirsty for more than the water from my well. At the end of that day, I knew that I was no longer trash, because he saw me as a treasure. I was respectable because he had valued me. I was good, because he had blessed me.

So I sit here, smiling still, even as the news of his death spreads. I hear the people talk, but there is so much that they still do not know.

And today, I do not think I will tell them just yet. I will keep my secret and savor it a while longer. There will be a time when those who despise me now will beg to hear my story – how Jesus came into a tainted land to find a tainted woman and replace her dark past with shining grace. Then they will see that his love is for all people – *all people.*

And I think they will remember me too…as the woman at the well.

Reflections on Photini

1. Because of her past, Photini's neighbors routinely shun her. How does she react outwardly to the treatment by her community?
2. Have you ever experienced what it means to be an outsider, especially in your own community? How did it feel?
3. Did you ever do something that was misunderstood by others who should have supported you? Have you ever been shunned because of a moral stance you took that was unpopular? Did you avoid these people, or did you find a way to make yourself understood?
4. How does Photini react to a stranger treating her like a friend? Might the fact that he was a Jew intensify this reaction?
5. How does Photini react to Jesus's revelation that he is the Messiah? How would you have reacted? Why does she believe him? Would you have believed him in her place?
6. How does Photini change during her encounter with Jesus? What might he have said that would engender this change?
7. Jesus treats Photini as a real person with a spark of divinity in her, no matter what she had done in the past. How can we model this behavior to our own communities, especially to the "outsiders"?
8. Jesus takes an unpopular road to reach Photini. Has God ever taken a difficult path to get to you? Did you realize this at the time? Do you see it now?
9. Even after she comprehends who Jesus is, Photini offers no excuses for her past. What can we learn from this behavior?
10. Photini plans to share her encounter with others. If you were in her place, how would you approach the people in her village, and how could you convince them to believe you?

Edra
Server of the Seder

In the house where the Last Supper took place, surely a woman was in charge of the dinner. Edra is an unquestioning servant for Jesus's inner circle, yet she is more than just a cook. As she quietly looks within, she stands for attentiveness to God's word and willingness to do his work.

My name is Edra, and it was here at the home I share with my husband and our three children that Jesus took his last supper.

Two nights ago, I cooked the Passover meal with the two sisters from Bethany, Yohanah, and some other friends. Jesus often had meals with us, so I found it strange that he wasn't planning to eat with our family – that he wanted a room apart. But we prepared our upstairs room for Jesus and his apostles as we were asked. When they arrived, I showed them in, lighting the lamps and placing the food and wine on the table. When I was sure they needed nothing more, I closed the door behind me.

Back at our family table, we said the ancient prayers, shared food and drink, and enjoyed happy conversation. Midway through our dinner, I decided to see if there was something more I could provide for the men upstairs. But Martha offered to go up to sit near the door in case they needed anything.

Near the end of our meal, I heard the back door of the upper room open and close. Judas rushed down the stairs and out the kitchen door without a word. Jesus often sent him on errands, so I thought this was just one more.

Not long after, Jesus came down, followed by the other men. He acknowledged no one, not thanking me in his usual gracious way. I thought this was strange, but it never occurred to me that I was looking at him for the last time.

The men of our group went out for their usual talk, and we women cleared our table and watched our children and grandchildren play. And then the men returned to say that Jesus had been arrested – betrayed by Judas! Even in my shock, I thought, *so...the errand.*

When my guests left and I was alone, I looked into the room where Jesus and his friends had eaten. We had not cleaned up that table. Having no heart for such a duty, I closed the door. Tomorrow is soon enough, I thought. I assumed Jesus would be imprisoned briefly and then released, as other holy men sometimes were. But tomorrow was not what I had hoped for.

On that tragic Friday – can it be just yesterday? – I began by doing normal things, trying with all my might to make things "ordinary" again. And of course, that was impossible.

By nightfall, I was weary, but I had one more job to do. I asked no one to help me clean the supper room. This was my obligation. No – this was my *honor*, my *privilege.*

The table was just as it had been when Jesus and the others were there – for the very last time. I sat where Jesus had sat, trying to feel some part of him still there. I thought about this gentle person who had shared food and time and love with our family. I remembered the little things – like the way he always found time to play with our children. And I cried.

After a while, I stood and looked at the scene before me. Plates of olives, bread crumbs, oil lamps long since burned down. One cup had been knocked over. The wine on the tablecloth looked like blood.

Then, as I started to clear the table, everything changed. I believe I felt his spirit within me. This man we had loved and followed was physically gone from us, but his *spirit* remained. He had told us to share what we had, to spread love and understanding, to care for each other. And now it was our responsibility to do that – even the women. Maybe *especially* the women.

As I finished my work, I prayed that the spirit of Jesus would remain. I closed the door on that room, but I knew that something had opened deep within me.

Reflections on Edra

1. Edra's home is always open to friends. Is your home like this? Who do you know who is like Edra in this way? How do you feel when you are at this person's house?
2. Why do you think Edra's house was chosen for this last meal? Was it just convenience? Coincidence? Or something else?
3. Edra finds it odd that Jesus doesn't want to share Seder with her family, yet she doesn't question his decision. Would you have done the same in her position?
4. When Judas leaves the house, she assumes Jesus has sent him on an "errand." Knowing that Jesus took a human form in order to die a human death, how does this change your perception of Judas's "errand"? If she had known what Judas was about to do, what might she have said to him?
5. When the men leave Edra's house, Jesus fails to thank her. This was unusual. Why did he do this? How do you think Edra felt about this? How would you have felt?
6. Do you think Edra had any premonitions about what was to happen next? What might have made her suspicious? Or was she just too caught up in serving dinner that she failed to notice the differences?
7. Have you ever "had a feeling" that something momentous was going to happen? Were you correct? How did you put the pieces together after the event? Did you say, "I should have known"?
8. Rather than asking friends to help her clean up the supper room, Edra chooses to do this alone. If she had asked *you* to help, what would your conversation have been like?
9. Edra sits where Jesus sat to feel closer to him. Have you ever done something like that? What did you do, and how did it make you feel?
10. At the end of the story, Edra feels a call to continue Jesus's work in some way. What about this woman might make her a good leader? Do you think we all have this call? In what ways can you lead?

Veronica
Offering the Veil

She is not mentioned in the gospels, but the woman with the veil has long been part of Christian writings. As Jesus carried his cross, Veronica stepped out of the crowd to perform a simple act of charity. She stands for courage, action against injustice, and embracing opportunities to do good.

There are days that change your life. The day you meet your best friend. The day you marry. The day your first child is born. And there are days that change the world. I believe yesterday was one of those.

Jerusalem is my home, but I travel with my merchant husband, so I'm not often here. When I came back for this visit, my mother told me that she had been very ill – and been *healed*. She told me that a new preacher, Jesus, had simply touched her. I only half-believed her, because my mother always exaggerates. She was so sure, though, and what mattered most was that she was now well.

It was only last Sunday when Jesus – the preacher, the healer – arrived in the city. I happened to be near the gates when he entered to shouts of "Hosanna." I saw him ride by on a donkey, while his people waved palm branches as if he were royalty. I watched, but I followed no further...until yesterday.

My mother's house is on a main street in the city. Friday morning, as we sat sharing tea, we heard an angry crowd approaching. Their shouts grew louder. We were completely unprepared for what we saw when we opened our door. *Jesus* was standing there, looking at us with pain in his eyes.

We had expected to see a neighborhood brawl or some drunken Roman soldiers, but there, directly in front of our house, was this healer! He had been savagely beaten. His eyes, nose, and mouth were swollen and outlined in red. Blood ran down his arms and legs. I had never beheld a man who looked like this.

After that endless moment, a soldier reached over and slammed our door shut. My mother began to cry. I settled her into bed with a cup of wine. When she fell asleep, I put on my veil and slipped out the door. I wasn't sure why. I just had to go.

I reached the crowd outside the city in the open road. I moved to the front of this awful procession so I could see the whole scene. And as Jesus moved closer, I believed that the pain in his eyes was defeat. Now, as I think back, I wonder if it was not defeat at all, but a kind of *triumph*, disguised by his own blood. We were all in disguise, I thought. Here in a crowd, we could all be invisible.

Jesus took another step, and then dropped to his knees under the weight of his cross. And suddenly I could no longer stand safely lost among this mass of people.

Some say it took courage to do what I did next. But they are wrong – I was compelled to do it by some power apart from my own. I pushed my way through the shouting people and rushed to his side.

I looked into his eyes, searching for permission to touch him. And in those eyes I saw my essence – not who I had always been, but who I became at that moment and would be forever. I gently put my hand to his cheek. He put his hand over mine. I held out my veil, and he pressed it to his face.

That was all. A soldier's rough hands pushed me down, but I felt nothing, heard nothing, as I sat in the dust with the veil cradled in my hands. I watched him until he turned away to follow the path to his death. I thought about following the crowd, but I did not. I had already experienced enough. I walked home slowly. Soon the noise faded, and by the time I reached my street, it was unnaturally quiet. A cold wind began to blow.

My mother was still asleep. I was relieved. I needed time to understand all this before I told her what I had witnessed. I lit a small lamp and sat on the floor. My mind was full, but my heart felt empty. My veil lay where I had dropped it. I picked it up and kissed it. As it fell open, I saw the gift he had left me. His face. There on my veil – *his face*.

I played the scene over and over in my mind. Why this gift? Why me? And I wondered...was I *chosen* to be part of this story? Or was my act as much a surprise to Jesus as it was to me?

Thunder shook me from my dreaming. Soon, a neighbor came to tell us all that had happened on the hill.

And now we will all go on, I suppose. Soon I will leave Jerusalem again, but something other than maps will guide me. Wherever this veil takes me, I will go. Whatever this veil requires of me, I will do.

Who I was before, I do not remember. But forever after, I will be his servant. And my name is Veronica.

Reflections on Veronica

1. Veronica is not part of the traditional four gospels, but her story is one of the Stations of the Cross and is mentioned in other holy books. Why do you think her story has endured despite lack of "publicity"? Is it just because of the veil?
2. Veronica was moved to action by the plight of Jesus. Of all the people who watched, no one else stepped forward. What kinds of qualities does such a person require?
3. How did most of the others in this crowd react to this procession? How might you have reacted? How do you think the crowd responded to Veronica's act?
4. Before the day of the crucifixion, Veronica had no personal contact with Jesus. What might have motivated her, first, to watch his suffering, and second, to act as she did?
5. Jerusalem as a violent place under the Romans, but Veronica was moved by this particular act of violence. What might have been different about it? Was the act itself different, or was Veronica different?
6. How do you think Veronica's life changed after that day? Do you think others treated her differently? Do you think she became different? Or more "herself"? In what ways?
7. What do you think Veronica did next? Do you think she joined Jesus's followers? What might the disciples and women have said to her?
8. We remember Veronica because of one action. She was important to Jesus because of her decision to respond as *he* would have responded. What do you think Jesus thought and felt when he saw her step forward? What might he have said?
9. Many of us feel moved when we see injustice, but few of us do anything about it. Does Veronica's decision and action make you feel differently? If we pray for and sympathize with victims of unjust treatment but do nothing else, are we still doing good?
10. Have you ever done something as brave and unexpected as Veronica's action? How did your friends and family respond? How did you feel? How did that moment change you? How did it change the person you helped?

Shulamit
Who Gave Sons to God

Salome, whose Hebrew name is Shulamit, is the mother of two apostles, James and John, and a relative of Mary of Nazareth. As one who has witnessed the beginnings and endings of many lives, she stands for service, optimism, and spiritual insight.

Life is a circle, like the sun coming up – there, over the hill. Birth to death, over and over, good to bad to good again. After the desolation of yesterday, surely the good must come again soon.

This house in Jerusalem is finally quiet. Mary and the other women are mercifully asleep – and my son John too. Zebedee, my husband, is in the north, fishing on the Sea of Galilee. My son James...I pray that he is safe. And Jesus is in his tomb. Can he be the farthest away of all?

Jesus has been part of my life for so long. I am Shulamit, one of his mother's family. Wasn't it just yesterday when Mary and I sat in her yard, watching those little boys at play? James, Jesus, and little John – they were so full of life! Sometimes when Jesus won a game, I would say, "Jesus, when you rule the world, be sure you have James and John with you. No army could defeat such power!" We would laugh, and Auntie Shula always got a big hug and kiss from Jesus.

And then they all grew up.

You may know that my husband runs the most successful fishing business in Galilee, with my older sons and even some hired men to help him. In such a man-centered household, it seems perfect that I am a midwife! It is so good to leave the noise and bustle of all those men to be with women and babies. So often, I've witnessed the intense courage of women, some even giving up their own lives so their children could live. God made women strong for good reason.

I was supposed to help Mary in birthing Jesus, but Joseph decided to take her to Bethlehem with him for that ridiculous Roman registration. "*Now*, Joseph?" I scolded. "Just *look* at her! What are you thinking?" But off they went, and they were gone for so long.

But by the time Jesus was walking and talking, they were back in Nazareth. And it was from Nazareth that Jesus came to Zebedee's boat and asked James and John to go with him as he started his preaching.

Zebedee was not happy, I can tell you! There was quite a scene – two of his sons, his best workers, going off with their carpenter cousin to do what? Wander and preach? Zebedee was even angrier when he heard that Jesus had also convinced Peter and Andrew, his fishing partners, to go too! How lucky I was to be called to a birth and miss all that arguing.

So they all went away. I'm so proud that my sons were with Jesus at all the important times of his life – the miracles, the healings, even his last night of prayer. I often think about what I said to Jesus about keeping James and John near him. If I had known...oh, I suppose I would have done nothing differently.

But the circle has turned again. Everything has changed in the last few days. We all feel lost now. I sit here, worn out from crying and soothing other women.

John and I will take Mary home to Nazareth soon, and we will go on somehow, around the circle once more. Life is for the living, we are told. But already I can feel changes coming, just as I read the signs in a woman's body before her baby arrives.

One woman's son dies, another is born. One day disappears, another takes its place. The sun sets, and the sun rises.

Let us see what tomorrow will bring.

Reflections on Shulamit

1. Shulamit sees life as a circle. Do you agree? In what ways have you seen life events form a circle?
2. As a kinswoman of Mary, Shulamit shared in Jesus's life from his early childhood. How would her relationship with the young Jesus be different from his relationship with his mother?
3. Do you have an "Auntie Shula"? Are you one yourself? How would you describe the relationship between a child and a favorite aunt?
4. As a midwife, Shulamit has a unique place in life's circle. How does her job of bringing life into the world affect her viewpoint? Has your own life been changed by the birth of a child – yours or someone else's? In what ways were you permanently changed?
5. Shulamit is philosophical about giving two sons to Jesus. She must have known that *his* fate would eventually be *their* fate. What do you think she was feeling and thinking as they left to follow him?
6. How do you think she dealt with her angry husband as her sons set off to change the world? What might this conversation have been like?
7. Shulamit was one of the women who stood on the hill as Jesus died on the cross. What feelings do you think she had in that moment? What might she have done or said to comfort the other women?
8. John, Shulamit's younger son, was also at the cross. What feelings might she have had about this young man, the only one of Jesus's apostles to witness his death? What might she have said to him?
9. In offering comfort to Mary, Shulamit shows sincere charity. Do you think she considers this act "charity"? Or is it simply the natural thing to do?
10. How do you deal with people who have lost loved ones in difficult ways? Have you ever been in the position of comfort-giver? How did you behave, and what things did you say?

Ruth
The Possessed

In the gospels, we learn that Jesus "casts out demons" from a woman. In healing Ruth, Jesus freed her – not just from inner darkness, but to become a defender of his new way. She stands for courage, victory with purpose, and resolve.

A shadowland was where I lived. Always an edge between me and the light, reminding me where I belonged.

"Possessed," some called me. They said I belonged to the devil. My world had both light and dark, but I never knew when the dark would overtake me. Try to imagine my life – never knowing when I would suddenly snap, shrieking curses and racing about, out of control. Waking from the darkness, my face in the dirt, people staring, with no knowledge of how it had happened. And hearing the voices of my parents – "Stop it, Ruth! You are scaring us! What sin have we committed to deserve this?" And the tears, so many tears. That was my world. Feared and fearful, alone in my difference. Seeking the light, afraid of the dark.

Then came the day when the two sides fought their final battle. I watched the darkness come for me, swaying, gliding, then crouching and leaping into me. I danced with it, fevered and wild-eyed. And then a voice...

"Come out of her!" a man commanded. A blinding light, a scream. Was it I who was screaming, or the darkness? And then I heard the darkness laugh. Yellow, green, orange spun before my eyes. I tasted salt and dust. I could not breathe, but the dance went on.

Again the man's voice – "Come out of her!" Light crashed painfully into my mind as the darkness tried to pull me back. A war was being waged inside me.

Then, nothing. Stillness. Peace. Exhaustion. I couldn't move. I didn't want to. Then I heard birds, wheels grinding in the street, astonished voices moving away. I looked up into the blue sky. Someone moved into view, kneeling beside me, brushing my hair from my face. I recognized the man called Jesus. "Your dance is over," he said. I breathed in the fresh air of my new world. And then he was gone.

A year has passed since Jesus healed me. At first, even my own family doubted that I was free from the seizures. Neighbors long accustomed to my unpredictable behavior were still wary. But after a time, people saw who I am now, cleansed and sane – the young woman who had always been there, but imprisoned in a body ruled by darkness.

And on this bright morning, I stand in the light, letting the sunshine and warmth wash over me. A month ago I was married, a dream that I had long since given up. The day was full of joy. My family celebrated, knowing that my darkness would not be an uninvited guest. The only dances were those I shared with my husband, my family, and my friends.

Where would I be if Jesus had not had compassion for me, had not seen my pain and fear, and stopped for that moment to challenge the darkness? Because he showed love and offered me grace, I can now be the woman that I longed to be and always truly was.

But news comes from Jerusalem that Jesus was killed for continuing the very acts of kindness like the one that healed me. It seems that men who proclaimed themselves "of the light" were truly dark in their spirits.

Do they think their darkness won? As Jesus was light to me, so will I be a light for him. I will tell my story. I will show people that *he is the light,* not just with my words, but with my life. Those of us who were touched by him will never lose this battle.

Reflections on Ruth

1. Ruth's "possession" may have been epilepsy or mental illness. But at this time, people didn't understand the meaning of these diseases. How does this make her healing even more impressive?
2. How did Ruth's family and community react to her condition? How do you think this affected Ruth? How do you think her personality was shaped by the words and actions of others?
3. How did Ruth deal with her condition? How do you think she changed over time, from when she was a child until the present?
4. Ruth compares her miracle to coming out of darkness into light. Have you ever had an experience like this? How did you make the transition? Who helped you? What was required of you to make this change?
5. Ruth describes her episodes as battles within her. How else might battles be waged in our bodies and spirits? What are some other ways to picture this? Would this apply to physical as well as mental disorders?
6. In many gospel stories, Jesus chooses people "on the edge," those who are somehow marginalized, to teach his lessons. Why do you think he did this? What is the common thread in these kinds of stories? What might his choices of "miracle recipients" mean?
7. Would people like Ruth become stronger representatives of Jesus than those who had simply heard his stories? In what way?
8. What can we learn from the way Ruth "became herself" as a result of her healing? How had her real self been suppressed? What might have happened to her if she had not been healed?
9. Some people who recover from illness simply wait for another disaster to befall them. Ruth uses her gift to make a beautiful life. Have you seen people react to difficulties in each of these ways? What made the responses so different? How might you react in such a situation?
10. Ruth resolves to tell her story. What might others say about it? What would she say or do to convince others that she had been healed?

Naomi
The Baker's Wife

Even in a city that was "holy," there were ordinary women. Naomi and her husband owned a simple bakery, but she was still part of the story of Jesus. She represents friendship, constancy, and charity.

In my neighborhood in Jerusalem, just one step takes you from the bustling street into a different world. That world is my husband Aaron's bakery, and it's not just a place to buy bread, but to hear the latest news and tell stories.

I am Naomi, the wife of that flour-covered man who stands over there at his work table. The men in Aaron's family have been bakers for generations. His hands work the dough lovingly, just as his ancestors did. Bread is the basis of life, they saw. With a little wine, you have a sustaining meal. It is that simple.

The Seder is just such a meal. When my neighbor, Edra, came to purchase bread for last Thursday's Passover dinner, she bought more than usual. She said that Jesus and his friends were sharing Seder with them. We had both been followers of this gentle man for some time. Edra chatted happily about the preparations as we walked to the market together.

But Friday morning, I heard frightened whispers in our shop and crying in the street. People said that Jesus had been arrested the night before, right after Seder. Some said the Jewish leaders were responsible. Others said it was the Romans. Someone else said that one of Jesus's own people had betrayed him.

Soon Edra came into our shop, sobbing, and told us that Jesus had already been tried and was to be crucified! She told me of the Passover meal and how Jesus had dismissed everyone but his closest friends. And she described how Judas had left in a great rush.

Edra and I sat for a while in silence, not knowing what to do except comfort each other. We decided to pray by working, as we did every other day. She went home, and I cleaned up for Aaron.

Later that night, after we learned how they had killed Jesus, I sat across the work-smoothed table from my husband. He stared at his hands. I reached over and took them into my own. We talked quietly of how Jesus's friends had come often to buy bread from us. "These hands," said Aaron, "they created the bread for Jesus's last meal on earth." And he put his head into those hands and cried. He looked up at me and said, "We are so blessed, Naomi. Blessed that we knew who he was and blessed that we could give him the bread that he needed."

"You and Jesus have strong hands," I told him. "Hands with a purpose. You use yours to make bread to nourish bodies. He allowed his hands to be nailed to a cross to nourish our souls."

We talked until this morning's dawn, Aaron and I. We remembered that Jesus had taught us to love each other, and in this way, to make a difference in the world. We will find a way to do this.

Hands can do so much. They can prepare a meal. Soothe a child. Caress a lover. Make a loaf of bread. And maybe even save a soul. We will try.

Reflections on Naomi

1. Naomi's bakery is a welcoming place. Do you know a place like this? How do you feel when you are there? How do the people who work there affect these feelings?
2. Naomi and Aaron have a loving marriage. Imagine a conversation between them on a very busy day in the shop. Contrast this with their conversation at the end of this story. What about their relationship allows each of these conversations to happen?
3. Naomi and Edra share their faith in Jesus openly. How does this compare to the stories of the women who were unable to do this? What does it mean to have a friend to share spiritual conversations with? Do you have such a friendship?
4. Bread is a frequent metaphor in religious stories. What are some similarities in this story to others?
5. Naomi "prays by working." How can everyday work be a prayer?
6. How does bread represent the simple things that we need to live? If bread were a virtue, how would you describe it?
7. Naomi knows what it means to be part of a grand plan. What would you ask her about this belief? What might she say to you?
8. When Naomi and Aaron realize what has happened, it is *she* who comforts *him*. How does she exemplify constancy and love? What might you have said or done to help Aaron understand his place in God's plan?
9. Hands are another theme in this story. What do they represent?
10. Naomi and Aaron are moved at the end to practice charity. Do you think they would have done the same without the drama of Good Friday? Do we all need some actual or spiritual event to motivate us?

Yohanah
A Disciple

The gospels call her Joanna. Yohanah left the palace of Herod to follow Jesus.
She used all her gifts to serve Jesus and the apostles, changing her life in the process.
She stands for responsiveness to God's call, bravery, intelligence, and self-knowledge.

I am so tired. It must be well past midnight. It feels like a thousand years since the last midnight – in this olive garden, where I sit now.

My name is Yohanah, and all that has happened is my fault. It was I who arranged the events that led Jesus to his death. Because of the plans I made, Jesus was in the wrong place at the wrong time.

I am a disciple, but different from the others. Yes, I am a woman, but there are other women in our little band of believers. But while most of them had little to leave behind, I left a palace to join Jesus – Herod's palace. My husband, Husah, is Herod's steward. I once wore soft silks and dined at feasts on velvet cushions. Now, I wear rough wools and eat barley soup on the hard ground.

I saw many things unfold in the great hall of the palace. Beautiful things... exotic entertainment and extravagant banquets. And terrible things...the murder of the Baptist. And I saw the pain in my husband's eyes when I told him I was leaving him to follow Jesus. Husah loved me so much that not only did he let me go freely, but he gave me money to take with me.

I was welcomed into Jesus's inner circle not because of that money, but because of the choice I had made to completely change my life. And I made myself useful. I had accompanied Husah to many towns to arrange for Herod's royal visits, and so I had connections. I knew innkeepers and merchants. It made sense for me to be the one who went ahead to set up lodgings and buy food. In this service, I worked with Jesus's own steward, a man who became my close friend – Judas.

And so it was I, the arranger of things, whom Jesus asked to plan the Seder on Thursday and to find a quiet place for him to pray afterward. That house was near Gethsemane, this garden he loved. Jesus didn't tell me not to tell Judas about the plan. So I did. After all, Judas was my partner, my companion – my *betrayer*. And so it was I who put Jesus in this place where the soldiers would find him.

I was still at the supper house when I heard of the arrest. I ran to Herod's palace when I heard Jesus had been taken there. I listened to Herod's vicious insults and watched as Jesus was dragged from the courtyard to Pilate. As I turned to follow, I looked up to my old window and saw Husah watching. I stepped away from the crowd so he would see me. We looked at each for a long moment, our hands raised in our secret sign of love. Then, I turned to go, my heart broken twice that night.

I found the other women of our group and together we waited for hours. And then we followed Jesus to the hill. All the men had run away except sweet, faithful John. And we women watched. We watched it all.

When we knew Jesus was dead, I came here to this beautiful, terrible garden. If I close my eyes and pray as he did, surely I will feel his spirit.

Come back, Lord... I need to serve you. Please come back and tell me what to do.

Reflections on Yohanah

1. Yohanah gives up comfort and a husband who loved her in order to serve Jesus. Have you ever had to give up something to maintain your faith?

2. Husah's deep love allowed Yohanah to accomplish great things, to play her part in the foundations of the early Christian church. Have you ever experienced a love so unselfish? Have you ever witnessed this in other relationships?

3. Yohanah chooses a strange life – to become a nomad in an obscure religious sect. How does she react to the change in her status? If you were her sister or friend, what would be your reaction?

4. How does Yohanah use her knowledge and skills to serve Jesus? How can you do the same thing?

5. Yohanah blames herself for Jesus's arrest, yet we know she was acting in accord with God's plan. Have you ever blamed yourself for something that was "God's idea"? How did you feel?

6. In his way, Judas was also doing God's will. How does Yohanah react to the actions of her close friend? If she'd had a chance to talk to him before or after his betrayal, what might they have said to each other?

7. What can we learn from the last sentence of the story? Is she doing the right thing by waiting instead of acting? Is it ever wrong to wait?

8. Would you consider Yohanah a revolutionary? Why or why not?

9. Yohanah chooses to put aside her past and concentrate on using her internal and external resources to act out God's plan for her. What kind of moral attributes did this require? Have you ever had to call on attributes like these?

10. Yohanah shows her deep faith by accepting a life of service, despite uncertainty and the disapproval of society. What hardships do women of faith face today, and what obstacles are in the way of our service? How does Yohanah serve as a role model for modern women?

Mary of Magdala
A Woman of Business

Many believe that Mary of Magdala was a "woman of the streets" before she was a disciple of Jesus. Maybe she had simply run her own business – which would have brought disapproval as well. But as Jesus's trust transforms her, she still knows how the world works. She stands for deep faith, realism, and self-sacrifice.

I have never been a woman who cries easily. When others slander me, I stand strong. "There goes Mary from Magdala," they say with contempt. "She can provide whatever you desire." But on a morning like this, I don't feel strong. I feel tears, and they are close. Tears of hurt, of guilt, of frustration – of *anger*.

It is so hard to think about what happened yesterday. It torments me to think of how he died. Nailed to a cross with common thieves! *They* may have deserved their fate, but what was *his* crime?

I am angry with myself, and I am angry with all his people. We could have saved him! And I should have known this! Am I not a businesswoman in a man's world? Do I not understand how these things are done? A word in the proper ear, coins pressed into a greedy palm, a promise to stay out of sight for a while, and all is forgotten. Could I not have redeemed his life with money as he redeemed my life with his love? But...would Jesus have allowed us to do this for him?

It seems so long ago when I first met him. I had come to the marketplace to see the goods that were being offered. A new bangle or piece of silk might catch my fancy. Maybe some spices, fruits and nuts, oil for my lamps. Vendors called to me, for I am a good customer. Women, jealous of my independence but ever ready to condemn, whispered as I passed, and as always, the men's eyes, not daring to meet mine, but always watching.

Yet no one saw the real me. I had long ago buried that unsure, desperate Mary who had walked out of a tiny fishing town long ago. They may have seen a self-reliant woman, but not the pain or the loneliness. So I held my head high, shaking off their stares and gossip just as I shook dust from my sandals. And then I felt something else – a deeper kind of watching. I turned to meet a pair of dark eyes different from the rest. I wondered what price he would ask for my attention, for everything comes at a price.

I looked at this man. He was dressed in plain brown robes and wore common sandals. Yet something about him did not seem to fit this ordinary appearance. I heard the men call him Master, and I realized that this must be Jesus, the preacher from Nazareth. His eyes continued to hold mine. He was looking *into* me, not *at* me. Finally, unable to bear the tension, I looked away. I – strong, capable Mary – felt weak! I took a step in retreat, but his voice stopped me. I turned again to face him. He was smiling gently. "You are Mary," he said, "and your sins are forgiven."

What? This was not what I had come to expect from men's lips. My sins? Forgiven? How could he do this? In his eyes, I saw something I could not comprehend. So I turned and ran, oblivious to the rude stares and derisive laughter of the people in the marketplace.

Soon I was home, in my sanctuary. I closed the door quickly, foolishly, as though that would keep his words outside. "Mary, your sins are forgiven," he had told me. And I cried. I remembered every offense that I had committed against God and the people in my life. When there were no more tears, I rose, hearing once again in my heart, "Mary, your sins are forgiven." And this time, I knew that it was true. I hurried back to the market, to this man who had changed my world.

Jesus was sitting with his friends in the shade of palm trees. The other men barred my way for a moment. At a word from him, they let me pass. I knelt and bowed my head, my hair covering his feet. I heard murmurs from the men, but I thought, "Let them have their small thoughts. I just want to be close to him." I felt his hand on my head, and I heard him whisper, "Sin no more." I had been lost in the world for so long, and no one had searched for me. I was right there, but no one ever saw the real me – until that day, when I was found, and loved, and freed. And from that day I was only his. He was the master of my heart and soul.

And now, on this deceptively lovely morning, I think of what I would have paid for his freedom! All I can do is wait and believe what he told us – that he will return and be with us always. Yes, I believe this, as much as I believe that he forgave my sins. I am holding tight to these words. And I will remain his most loyal and patient servant, no matter what the price may be.

Reflections on Mary of Magdala

1. Does this story of Mary of Magdala match your former ideas about her, or is it different? In what ways?
2. Mary considers herself first and foremost a businesswoman, and legends tell us that her family had quite a successful fishing business. How does this make her different from other women of the time? Do you think she treated "ordinary" woman differently?
3. She grew up in a small fishing village but now lives apart from her family in a crowded city. Have you ever had to change your lifestyle this radically, or do you know someone who has? What strengths might this lead to?
4. Mary recalls the day she met Jesus. How did her reaction to him change in such a short time? What do you think made the difference to her?
5. Mary is angry with herself because she didn't step in to ransom Jesus. If she had done this, would things have been different? Why or why not?
6. Mary is realistic. She looks life in the face and does what is needed. How was she a model for women of her time? For women of today?
7. How do you think the apostles reacted to Jesus's acceptance of Mary into the inner circle? What might these men have said to each other about her?
8. How do you think Mary interacted with other women who were close to Jesus? Imagine a conversation between her and Yohanah or one of the mothers or wives of the apostles. What might they say to each other? How would this conversation change after Jesus's death?
9. Mary says she was "lost, and no one had searched" for her. Have you ever felt this way? How were you "found"? How did the event change you?
10. Imagine a scene between Mary of Magdala and Jesus's mother on the day after the crucifixion. What might they have said?

Cyborea
Mother of the Betrayer

There was another mother who mourned her son on Good Friday. We know her only because of her child – Judas. She is conflicted by despair, hope, and confusion, yet she stands for constancy and unconditional love.

When I look at the night sky, I see silver. Silver moon. Silver stars. Silver coins.

Do you have any silver? Hold a few coins in your hand. They are cold, are they not? Even the light that reflects from them is cold. As cold as death. As cold as eternal loneliness.

My name is Cyborea, and I am of the tribe of Reuben. I live in this little street of poor families. You need not remember me, but you will never forget my son. His name is Judas.

It is only two days since I last saw him. That evening, my neighbors had joined me here in Jerusalem for the Passover meal. Most of us have little, and our children are grown and gone, so we often share meals. After dinner, with the other women, I was cleaning up. There had been a lot of noise in the street, unusual for that time of night, and the men had left to see what was going on. They were slow in returning, but we women were busy, so it did not seem so long.

Then Benjamin, the husband of Sarah, my best friend, opened the door. He was breathing hard. "Where is Judas?" he said to me sharply. "He is with the Master," I said. Why? Is something wrong?"

Such a simple question...*Is something wrong?* Yes, something was very wrong indeed.

"Jesus has been arrested," Benjamin said, his eyes full of fury. I heard shocked gasps and cries from the women behind me. "Have the others been arrested too?" I asked. "Has Judas..." I could not finish. Had the Romans taken them all?

"No," said Benjamin. "But they are saying that Judas was the cause of this!"

The room was suddenly silent. This could not be! Judas was so close to Jesus. But if they had taken Jesus, surely Judas was there when it happened. Was Benjamin saying that Judas was somehow at fault?

I turned to Sarah. Surely, she could not accept a story like this. But she looked only at her husband, and without a word to me, stepped quickly out my back door. The others left with her. I was alone.

I sat on my bench by the window. I lit a candle and prayed: "Dear God of heaven and earth, protect my son. Please bring him home to me. I love him so very much."

I forced my mind go over what I knew to be the truth. Judas *loved* Jesus. He had changed his life to be with him. I could see no possible way that he could have caused Jesus's arrest. The men must be wrong. I opened the door and looked down the street, half expecting to see Judas. He would come home and explain everything.

I sat by the window all night, waiting. But the street stayed empty. No one seemed to be alive here except me. My oil lamp burned down and flickered out, but still I kept watch. I thought about my son. I remembered the day that he had first seen Jesus. He had almost flown into the house and said, "Mother, you must come to hear this amazing man!" And so, of course, I went. I wanted to see this rabbi who would surely shape my son's future, maybe even give a noble purpose to his life.

They are the same age, you know, Jesus and Judas. They had so much in common. And now, with this new movement, they had new ideas to talk about, new ways to see the world! Jesus brought Judas into his inner circle – the only one who was not from Galilee. I was so proud. He was in charge of their money, buying food, distributing alms, collecting gifts. I think he was the one Jesus trusted most. So how did we get to this black place?

I waited up all night, but Judas never came home. As I sat by my window, unseen at first light, I heard people talking in the street. Jesus had been taken to Pilate and then to Herod. The Twelve had scattered. And I heard my son's name over and over. I closed the window then and lay on my bed. My thoughts turned to Mary, the Master's mother. How she must be suffering! I would go to her, but would she let me near her?

And Friday morning, I went to the market early, searching for Judas. No one would look at me. The baker gave me my bread but waved away my coins as if they were cursed. People whispered as I passed. Yet I had done nothing wrong – nothing except to be the mother of Judas. And so I went home and again sat here, watching from the window for my son.

By noon, it seemed as if my whole neighborhood had deserted the streets to see what was happening to Jesus. I stayed home. What would Judas think when he came back and did not find me here?

So it was again dark when Sarah came to my door. She said, "I have terrible news. They have killed Jesus!" But if they had killed Jesus, then...*my son too?*

"And Judas?" I asked, with the last of my hope. "He is gone," Sarah said softly, her tears now flowing with mine.

Brave Sarah – she told me the whole story. The betrayal. The kiss. The coins. The cross. The tree. And then she went home, and I have not moved since.

No women will come to comfort me. No community will mourn my dead child. Oh yes, my Judas will be remembered, not for the good son he was, but as the man who gave up Jesus to his murderers.

So I will wrap myself in black and sing the songs of mourning by myself. When the families light prayer candles, our names will not be mentioned. The love I bear for my son will always set me apart.

No one should have to mourn alone. Perhaps *you* could stay with me for a while... but no, that is too much to ask. This is my burden – only mine.

May God help us all.

Reflections on Cyborea

1. Given Judas's high place in Jesus's circle, Cyborea had a well-founded pride in her son. He was a trusted friend, a leader among the Apostles. This made his fall even more dramatic. What might be a good example of someone whose life might parallel the life of Judas? Put yourself in that person's mother's place. How would you feel? How would you react to the rejection?
2. Try to imagine Cyborea's sense of confusion at the moment when she is told her son has done the unthinkable. Have you ever been faced with news about a loved one that "can't be true"? What were your first reactions? Were you outraged? Hurt? Sick? How did you handle this? Did you look for help? From whom?
3. Cyborea is perhaps the only person in history to continue to love Judas after the betrayal. Have you ever been the only one to support someone whom others had abandoned? Did you keep this private, or did you let others know how you felt? What was the reaction?
4. Cyborea prays, but she has few words to say. It's been said that it's better to have a heart without words than words without heart. When have you prayed without words? How did this help you?
5. As many mothers have done, Cyborea waits up all night for a son to come home. What might she have done if he had come back? What might she have said if he had told her what he had done? What would you have done?
6. Cyborea remembers that Mary has also lost her son. Imagine that the two women met at some time. What might they have said to each other?
7. The next morning, people had already placed blame on Cyborea for the acts of her son, though she had done nothing wrong. Have you ever had to bear the ill will of others for something you haven't done? How did you feel? What might you have said to these people?
8. In the end, Cyborea is alone. Do you think she ever recovered from her despair? Who might have brought her comfort? How long would it have taken for her to be accepted again, if ever? Do you know someone whose despair and sense of loss was as overwhelming? How did this person deal with the circumstances? How would you act in this position?
9. There must be a "sisterhood" of mothers of men who have done terrible crimes, such as those on death rows of prisons. Imagine yourself in a prison visitors' room filled with mothers waiting to visit their sons. What might the conversation be like? If you were one of these women, what would you say to the others?
10. Do you think any of the other women in this book eventually may have come to Cyborea to comfort her? Which ones? What might they have said to her?

Mary of Nazareth
His Mother

Beyond the near-divinity ascribed to Mary, she was a real woman. When God asked her for dedication not just spiritually but physically, not just within her private soul but in public view, she said yes. She stands for acceptance, complete trust in God, understanding, and womanly strength.

You are here, my Lord God. I hear your voice – "Mary, I will give you the strength." That is what you have always said to me.

I sit in this house in Jerusalem as the gentle dawn brushes away last night's awful darkness. I remember the first time I heard you. I was a little girl, and my mother had asked me to watch my baby sister. As we played, I heard a hushed voice say, "I will give you the strength." Turning to see who was speaking and seeing no one, I assumed that it was one of my uncles playing a trick. But the sound of the words stayed with me.

Over the years, you would whisper those reassuring words in my days and nights, reinforcing that first promise. I told no one what I heard. Prayerfully, I asked who was talking to me. And you answered me, saying you were the Father God. You told me that you loved all your children on earth, but that I was *special*. That I would bring great joy to the world and great sorrow to myself, but that you would always protect me.

Then, when the angel told me that I would be the mother of your son, I was afraid. I was so young – I hardly knew what this meant! But you calmed my fright. And because of your voice, I could hold my head up, protected from the sting of gossip and stares when my body showed what was happening to me, because I knew the truth about the child that I carried. When I cried in the stable with the pain of childbirth, your voice gave me comfort. What had I to fear if you were with me? You guided me as I raised my son from a baby to a young man. And when Jesus left my home to preach, your voice sustained me.

I remember that day on a hillside, when I went to Peter and said, "Tell Jesus that his mother and family are here." Jesus looked at me, but spoke only to Peter, saying, "Who is my mother?" The intensity of this question and the bluntness of the words stung me, but I felt your calming presence. I smiled at my family and said, "He is just reminding us of who he is." I looked into my son's eyes for a moment and saw...what? An apology? Sorrow? Resignation? Gratitude? Farewell?

But until these last days, I never fully understood the meaning, the depth of the strength you always gave me. Those other struggles were of my worldly life, but this one is of my spirit, and I need you now more than ever before.

As I watched them hang my son on a cross, your voice was like an embrace, a support that nothing on earth could give me. And as my Jesus died, I remembered that he had never been simply my earthly son. For a time, he had been mine to love and care for, but he would not be there to love and care for me as I grew old. When he said to John, "This is your mother now," I knew that Jesus was no longer mine – that he was every person's son, brother, and friend.

My tears then were for the complete, absolute loss that I was feeling. Strength was for tomorrow. Now I was just another woman who had lost her son, and you allowed me to feel that human grief. I felt your presence and love surround me, repeating your promise without the need to ask.

What love you must have for me, Father God. From the very beginning, you nurtured me, protected me with your voice, encouraged my confidence to grow. I have become strong because you have *made* me strong. And today, I can bear even this terrible sword in my heart. I know there is a promise that he will return, but it seems impossible after what I saw yesterday. That hope will wait, along with the rest of living.

So now I will go into the next room to sit with the mourners. I will weep with the other women and allow them to comfort me as I comfort them. And then we will prepare the spices and balms for anointing my son's body.

But beneath it all, and until I die, I will listen for your soft voice telling me, "I will give you the strength." And I am so grateful for the life you chose for me.

Reflections on Mary of Nazareth

1. Traditionally, we think of Mary only as Jesus's mother. But she was a real woman first. What "womanly" virtues does she model for us? Start with strength.

2. From her childhood, Mary knew that God would always give her the strength she needed. Does God do this for all of us? Was there ever a time when you felt that you did not have the strength you needed? What did you do? How did this change you?

3. Mary used strength and faith to say "yes" to whatever God sent her, including a surprise pregnancy. What is the hardest request that you've ever had to accept from God? How did you feel about it? What was the result? Were you afraid? Did you have regrets?

4. Being the mother of Jesus was not easy! What expectations do you think Jesus's followers had of Mary? Do you think anyone ever used her to get nearer to Jesus? Would this have been good or bad? What other problems do you think were caused by her close relationship to her son?

5. Many mothers would have been insulted by a remark like the one Jesus said on the hillside. How does Mary respond, and what does this say about her faith and love? Imagine yourself in the same place. What might you have said or felt? What do you think others said to each other when they heard this comment?

6. Mary says she sees something in Jesus's eyes when he says, "Who is my mother?" Which of the emotions do you think he was trying to convey – remorse, sorrow, resignation, gratitude, farewell – or something else?

7. Mary went through many of the same difficulties of all the other women in this book – with one difference. She *knew* what was coming, or at least had an idea of it. How would this have made her life as Jesus's mother harder? Easier?

8. At the cross, Mary says, "I knew he was no longer mine." What does she mean? Have you ever felt this way about a child, a parent, or a friend? What did you feel? How long did the feeling last?

9. Even with her piety, Mary has to struggle to keep her hope alive. When you have been in a position where all seemed lost, what kept you going? What did you have to do to get through it?

10. In the end, Mary turns to her friends, realizing that she will not only have to receive their comfort, but give it as well. How are women different in this regard? What allows women to share deep feelings and support each other even as they need to be supported? When has this happened to you? How did it strengthen you?

Ways to Use These Readings

Group study and discussion
The questions that follow each woman's story can generate valuable discussion when used in study groups. After reading the story aloud, groups can use some or all of the questions to spark discussion and evoke deep feelings. They could also be the basis of a weekend retreat.

Private reflection, with or without journaling
These stories can also become the basis of a personal spiritual journey during Lent or at any other time of the year. The questions present opportunities to explore feelings, memories, and intentions.

Dramatic presentations, singly or in groups
The impact of presenting the readings dramatically is *powerful.* Whether the stories are memorized or read, the effect of "seeing and hearing" one of these women is proven to be deeply moving. The presentation can be simple, without costuming, or as detailed as a theatrical performance.

Some suggestions for simple presentations:
• One or more women can sit or stand at front of the room.
• A group of women can enter together and sit at various places, each rising to tell her story from different vantage point.
• In a candlelit church or room, a woman can enter from the rear or side, or perhaps from a pew or chair where she has sat unnoticed. Or she may begin to speak as soon as she appears, and walk among the audience as she tells her story.

Suggestions for presenting the entire group:
The entire group can be presented at one time. The women can enter singly or in small groups to take their seats on 24 chairs in a semicircle. Then, one by one, they tell their stories. Some may interact silently with each other or react to the stories in their own way.

Costuming suggestions:
The readings can, of course, be read in modern dress, but costumes can add to the effect. Choir robes or other draped garments are a good base, and veils and scarves are easy to incorporate.

Based on what we know of these women and other women of their time, here are some ideas for costumes:

Claudia, the wife of Pontius Pilate. Around 25; wears a toga with a brooch at her shoulder, perhaps a circlet of gold on her head; her hair is uncovered, worn up or in curls.

Cyborea, the mother of Judas. In her 50s; dressed in black with a thick veil covering her hair; no jewelry; may be holding some silver coins.

Deenah, one of those who shouted for the crucifixion of Jesus. Any age; wears a plain robe and veil to makes her look as ordinary as possible.

Edra, hostess of the Last Supper. Late 30s or early 40s; in a simple "housewife's" robe and a plain veil tied at the back; may be holding a dinner napkin.

Elisheva, mother of John the Baptist. About 65; wears a plain robe and no jewelry; brown or gray veil.

Ellori, one of the lepers whom Jesus healed. Late 20s; to show that she is now healthy, wears a sleeveless or short-sleeved robe; hair uncovered.

Halima, the wife of Simon of Cyrenia. Early 30s; wears a bright robe with a small turban or scarf; large silver earrings.

Kitra, the servant of Caiaphas. In her mid-teens; may have braided hair; wears a simple shift; a slave bracelet on her upper arm.

Martha of Bethany, sister of Mary and Lazarus. In her late 20s, sturdy but stately; her hair is totally hidden; no jewelry; simple but not shabby robe.

Mary of Bethany, Martha's sister. Early or mid-20s; wears her hair loose with no veil; bright fabric; simple jewelry.

Mary of Magdala, Jesus's companion and disciple. Late 20s; silk robe and gold earrings; hair is loose beneath a sequined veil.

Mary of Nazareth, Jesus's mother. About 45; wears an ordinary shift and shawl, may be blue; one or two veils; no jewelry.

Naomi, the baker's wife. Mid-to-late 30s; wears a white robe and apron; hair is tied back with a short veil; may be carrying a loaf of bread wrapped in cloth.

Perpetua, the wife of Peter. Early 30s; wears a dark robe; short veil; sleeves are rolled back to show strong arms.

Photini, the woman at the well. About 30; as she is a Samaritan, her robe should be different from the women of Judea; her hair may be in braids; lots of jewelry.

Rachael, the widow. In her 50s or 60s; wears a shabby black robe and simple black veil; may be carrying a small bag of coins.

Rafca, the bride from Cana. Late teens; wears bright robes and a veil far back on her loose hair; jingling, "happy" jewelry.

Ruth, who had been possessed. About 25 to 30; wears a dark robe and perhaps a striped veil; simple jewelry.

Shoshanna, the innkeeper's wife. Possibly 55 to 65; hair is free under a loose veil; no jewelry.

Shulamit, mother of the apostles James and John. In her 50s; wears her hair tied back under a veil; simple robe of any color, sleeves pushed back.

Talit, the little girl raised from the dead. Mid-teens; long hair worn loose over a simple, youthful robe; small jewelry; may be carrying a Jewish prayer shawl.

Tovah, the mother of the boy with loaves and fishes. About 25; wears a robe with a shawl tied across one shoulder; veil far back on her hair; may be carrying a basket.

Veronica, the woman who offered her veil to Jesus. Late 20s; "richer" robe as she has traveled; hair is loose and uncovered; may be carrying a white veil.

Yohanah, a disciple of Jesus. Late 20s or early 30s; wears a well-worn robe and veil covering most of her hair; no jewelry.

<u>Grouping suggestions:</u>
To present all 24 women at once, we recommend the order used in this book. But if smaller groups are more appropriate, these are logical groupings.

- The family of Jesus: Mary of Nazareth, Shulamit, Elisheva, Rafca
- Closest women friends of Jesus: Mary of Bethany, Martha, Mary of Magdala, Yohanah
- Disciples and relatives of apostles: Perpetua, Cyborea, Shulamit, Yohanah, Mary of Magdala
- Those who were healed by Jesus: Ellori, Ruth, Talit
- Those who learned of Jesus through his actions: Rachael, Edra, Tovah, Naomi
- Those who didn't know about Jesus until Holy Week: Veronica, Halima, Deenah, Kitra, Shoshanna
- Non-natives of Judea: Claudia, Photini, Halima
- Those who witnessed miracles: Mary of Nazareth, Mary of Magdala, Mary of Bethany, Martha, Rafca, Ellori, Ruth, Talit, Tovah, Veronica
- Those who witnessed the crucifixion: Mary of Nazareth, Mary of Magdala, Shulamit, Halima, Deenah, Ellori, Yohanah
- The youngest: Talit, Rafca, Kitra
- The oldest: Elisheva, Shoshanna, Rachael

As sermon themes or readings during a service, especially Lent
These readings can serve as effective focal points for individual sermons. They can also be used as themes in a sequence for Lenten services. Taken separately, the readings can be used to demonstrate or exemplify certain virtues, life choices, or human interaction. They present new vantage points for contemplating the life of Jesus. Examples:

Claudia – Justice, insight, acceptance of God's will
Cyborea – Constancy, unconditional love
Deenah – Self-knowledge, self-acceptance, self-forgiveness
Edra – Attentiveness to divine direction, willingness to do God's work
Elisheva – Unwavering friendship, faithfulness, optimistic trust in God's plan
Ellori – Gratitude, trust in God's forgiveness
Halima – Devotion, understanding, courage to face challenges
Kitra – Loyalty, courage, truth
Mary of Magdala – Deep faith, realism, self-sacrifice
Mary of Bethany – Joy in the present, thankfulness, equality, faith in God's plans
Mary of Nazareth – Acceptance, trust in God, understanding, womanly strength
Martha – Patience, trust, realizing our worth in God's sight
Naomi – Friendship, constancy, charity
Perpetua – Fierce faith, compassion, willingness to change
Photini – Intelligence, self-acceptance, equality, good humor
Rachael – Self-reliance, abiding faith, charity
Rafca – Joy, wonder, optimism, gratitude

Ruth – Courage, victory with purpose, resolve
Shoshanna – Unquestioning love, active charity, sisterhood
Shulamit – Service, optimism, spiritual insight
Talit – Complete confidence in eternal life, simple faith, cheerful resilience
Tovah – Belief, the ability to change, the value of giving
Veronica – Fearlessness, action against injustice, embracing chances to do good
Yohanah – Responsiveness to God's call, bravery, intelligence, self-knowledge

Groups of women may be also used as study focuses for the six weeks of Lent
Week One: *Elisheva, Mary of Bethany, Rafca, Shoshanna*
Week Two: *Ellori, Ruth, Talit, Tovah*
Week Three: *Shulamit, Rachael, Photini, Martha*
Week Four: *Yohanah, Veronica, Perpetua, Naomi*
Week Five: *Mary of Magdala, Edra, Claudia, Kitra*
Week Six: *Deenah, Halima, Cyborea, Mary of Nazareth*

A Guided Meditation on the Women

This exercise is designed as a *relaxing, healing, prayerful experience* for those who are already familiar with the readings. A good setting would be a quiet room with low light or candles, with enough room between people to give a feeling of space. The reader should use a soft, soothing voice and resist the urge to rush. Take time for listeners to internalize and react privately to the words. After the reading, allow participants to leave as they wish; some may want to sit quietly for a few minutes. This can also be used as a private prayer to "stay in touch" with the women of the readings.

Close your eyes and breathe naturally for a few moments. Try to quiet your thoughts. Relax and step away from your worries for just a while.

Then, imagine yourself sitting in a beautiful, shaded garden. You feel a gentle breeze from the trees and hear the leaves rustle. It's warm, and you can smell the perfume of the flowers all around. It's very, very peaceful.

Now, you become aware that you are not alone. You are in the center of a circle of women, with 24 beautiful faces all focusing on you.

You realize that they are not strangers. You know them well. They are some of your best friends. As you look at them, you see that each one has a gift for you.

One by one, they step forward to give you their gifts.

- The first woman is one of the oldest. She wears a light robe, and her head is covered with a brown veil. Her face is lined, but the lines have come from smiling. She is Elisheva, Mary's aunt. She has been Mary's steadfast friend, and she is yours, too. She offers her gift to you. It is companionship, faithfulness, and cheerful certainty that God's plan works for our greatest good. You take the gift.
- As Elisheva returns to the circle, a young girl takes her place. Her dark hair is loose, and it falls in long curls over her pink robe. Her face glows as she comes close to you. This is Talit, the girl Jesus brought back from death. She is very happy to give you her gift – the confidence that comes from belief in eternal life, simple faith, and youthful resilience no matter how dark things seem to be. You take the gift.
- A tall woman takes Talit's place before you. Her robes are scarlet and gold, and her hair is bound in a white turban. This is Halima from Cyrenia. She watched as her husband helped Jesus to carry his cross. She is here to help you to bear whatever burdens you have today. She offers her gift to you. It is the devotion of lifelong friends, understanding of the present, and the courage to face challenges. You take the gift.
- The next woman is dressed in gray and black. She is small, and older than most of the others. She doesn't smile, but you still feel her connection to you. This is Rachael, the widow. She is used to being alone and taking care of herself. She is

the one who gave all that she had to the poor, even though she was poor herself. She holds out her gift. It is self-reliance, abiding faith in God, and the ability to give and receive charity. You take the gift.

- As Rachael steps back, you see a young woman with a dazzling smile and a delicate green veil that matches her eyes. She seems confident and positive. She is Mary of Bethany, who watched as Jesus brought her brother Lazarus out of his tomb. She knows that God answers prayers. She offers her gift to you. It is joy in the small moments of the present and past, thankfulness for every blessing, a sense of being entitled to God's mercy, and deep faith. You take the gift.

- The next woman is beautiful in a far different way. She wears a toga in the Roman style, with a jeweled brooch at her shoulder. There is a circlet of gold on her auburn hair. She is the Lady Claudia, wife of Pontius Pilate. She tried but failed to save the life of Jesus. She offers you her gift. It is belief in divine justice, trust in her own insight, and acceptance of God's will. You take the gift.

- The young woman who steps up now has an aura of warm exuberance. She is round, from her brown eyes to her pink cheeks to her blossoming body. This is Rafca. Jesus and his friends danced at her wedding in Cana, enjoying the finest wine the world has ever known. Every day, she remembers how blessed she was to have a personal miracle. She holds out her gift. It is joy in memories, wonder in the magnitude of God's gifts, optimism, and gratitude for every day. You take the gift.

- The next woman approaches slowly, as if you might refuse what she offers. She looks plain, but her eyes hold deep emotion. This is Deenah. She stood in the crowd in Jerusalem and called for crucifixion with so many others. It has taken a long time, but she has finally found peace within herself. She holds out her gift. It is self-knowledge, self-acceptance, and self-forgiveness. You take the gift.

- A woman dressed in brown comes forward. Her hair is hidden by her white veil, and her sleeves are rolled up to show strong arms. When she smiles at you, you feel protected. This is Perpetua, Peter's wife. As a fisherman's woman, she knew the beauty and pain of hard work. And as his true partner, she stood by her husband on his darkest night. She presents her gift. It is fierce faithfulness, compassion, and the willingness to change when God asks. You take the gift.

- The next woman is tall and thin, and she approaches you cautiously. She isn't used to coming forward in front of a group. She is Martha, Mary of Bethany's sister. She wears a plain robe, and her hair is tied back beneath her veil. She served Jesus without being seen, yet she loved him as much as the rest of these women. She holds out her gift. It is patience, contentment in service, and the realization that God sees us all equally, as beloved daughters. You take the gift.

- An older woman in the circle comes forward. She is small and sturdy, and her gray hair flows free under a linen veil. She smiles at you, and you feel comfort in that smile. This is Shoshanna, from the inn at Bethlehem. It was in her stable that Jesus was born. She knows that all good acts are repaid, and that God forgets nothing. She has a gift for you. Her gift is unquestioning love, active charity, and the bond of sisterhood. You take the gift.

- The next woman looks neither old nor young. She wears no veil, and the sleeves on her robe are short. This is Ellori, and she knows what it means to be very sick and then recover. She is one of the lepers healed by Jesus, and her bare arms reassure her that she is truly well. She has a gift for you. It is gratitude, the hope of healing, and trust in the power of God's forgiveness. You take the gift.

- Now, a girl in her teens comes to you. She has dark, braided hair, and she wears a simple shift. On her upper arm is a slave bracelet. She is Kitra, and she works in the household of Caiaphas, the high priest. She was with Peter on the night Jesus was arrested. In her way, she defended Jesus when Peter could not. She has a gift for you. She offers you loyalty, courage, and the strength to face the truth. You take the gift.

- A pretty young woman carrying a basket moves toward you. She wears a dark blue robe with a shawl tied across one shoulder. This is Tovah. She has a small son who, one day, with the blessing of Jesus, shared his lunch with five thousand people. She knows about surprises, and how they can be seen as good and bad. She holds out her gift. It is the ability to believe the unbelievable, willingness to change when change is good, and the value of giving. You take the gift.

- The woman who comes up now has many braids, tied with bright cords. Her dress is crimson, and it hangs carelessly from her shoulders. She looks at you directly with beautiful dark eyes, as if daring you to dismiss her. She is Photini of Samaria, the woman who gave Jesus water from her well. She is the first "outsider" who really knew who he was. She wears this privilege like a jewel. She has a gift for you. Her gift is confidence in her own intelligence, self-acceptance, and a touch of humor at the inequities of life. You take the gift.

- You feel that you have known the next woman at some time in your life. She is dressed simply, her hair tucked under a short veil. She is one of many Jewish women who were part of the fabric of Jerusalem. She is Edra, and it was her home that Jesus and his friends chose for their final Seder dinner. She has a gift for you. Edra's gift is attentiveness to divine direction, willingness to do God's work, and calm when all seems to be chaos. You take the gift.

- A tall, pale woman approaches you. She wears a simple white robe with a blue sash, and there is a white veil in her hand. Her hair is curly, and it hangs loose, uncovered. She nods, graciously, yet seriously. She is Veronica, the woman who passed by the Roman soldiers to offer her veil to Jesus as he carried his cross. She knows how it feels to defy the odds when your goal is goodness. She has a gift for you. It is fearlessness, the will to act against injustice, and the strength to embrace chances to do God's will. You take the gift.

- The woman who comes next has a wide smile in a maturing face, sparkling eyes, and a strong body. In a plain robe with her hair tied back in a single braid, she makes you feel safe by her simple presence. This is Shulamit, mother of the apostles James and John, and a member of Jesus's family. As a midwife, she eased many women's pain and saw many new lives come into the world. As a devoted friend, she stood by Mary as they watched Jesus die. She has a gift for you. She gives you joy in service to others, optimism, and spiritual insight. You take the gift.

- A small woman comes forward. Her head is down, but she looks up at you with joy and hope. She wears a dark robe and a striped veil. She smiles shyly, but with compassion. This is Ruth. Once she was possessed by darkness, lonely in a world that no one else understood. Jesus set her free. She has a gift for you. It is courage, the knowledge that victory requires repayment, and resolve to make a beautiful life of what is given to you. You take the gift.

- The next woman is familiar, in the way that many strangers feel familiar. She is short, plump, and has an open, welcoming face. She wears a plain white robe and a big apron. This is Naomi. Her husband baked the bread that Jesus and his friends ate at his last supper on earth. She knows what it means to be part of God's great plan. She has a gift for you. It is caring friendship, constancy, and charity. You take the gift.

- The woman who comes to you now is dressed in a simple gray robe and veil, but she wears it like a queen. Her skin and hair are smooth and soft, and she walks with grace. This is Yohanah, and she once lived in the palace of Herod. She left her silks and jewels to follow Jesus. She also knows the hardships that can come with giving your life completely to him. She holds out her gift. It is responsiveness to God's call, bravery, intelligence, and the ability to question your decisions. You take the gift.

- The next woman who stands before you is tall and strong. She is beautiful, in a yellow robe and gold earrings, her hair loose beneath a white veil. She is Mary of Magdala, the woman from a fishing village who became one of Jesus' closest companions. She has come a long way, from poverty to success to disdain, and now to resolve. She wants to give you a gift. She offers you a deep, unshakable faith, realism, self-sacrifice, and the power to turn righteous anger into good. You take the gift.

- There is a pall of sadness around the next woman. It covers her black robes and veil almost visibly. Her smile is sad, and she looks at you with questions in her eyes. This is Cyborea. She is the mother of Judas. She knows how it feels to fall from grace in the eyes of others, and she knows the pain of loving the unlovable. She holds out her gift. It is constancy and unconditional love. It is strength even in the dark. You take the gift.

- The last woman comes forward. She is small and slight, and she looks very much like the others. But under the blue veil, her face glows with its own light. Her eyes draw you in, away from all pain and worry. This is Mary of Nazareth, the mother of Jesus. She has been through many of the same things as the other women, but she saw it all coming. Even knowing what awaited her, she always said yes to God's way. She steps close to you and places a gift in your hand. It is pure faith, complete trust, tranquility, and the peace in knowing that God has our life planned and that his plan is good. You take the gift.

Now, you look around the entire circle, at each face filled with love for you. With all their gifts surrounding you, you are now part of their sisterhood. Rest with a soft, clear mind, knowing that these women will always be as close to you as they are now.

In Gratitude

We gratefully acknowledge our appreciation to our friends and families:

To Cathy Ake, pastor of First United Methodist Church of New London, Ohio, for being the first minister to welcome "our girls" to join her services and express themselves "in person" to her congregation.

To Chad-Michael Simon for his inspiring cover.

To Jim Anderson, for encouraging us to share our work with the world.

And to our best friends, who know who they are, for their loving support.

About the Authors

Longtime friends Veronica Hughes and Deborah Landis began writing these stories more than a decade ago, at first as monologues to present at Lenten services at Debbi's church in New London, Ohio. Over the years, the authors worked at Debbi's country kitchen table to channel the stories of more women, to allow them to speak the words that were never heard and to craft a more holistic, realistic picture of what the first Holy Week might have been like. For Veronica and Debbi, "the girls" became true friends.

Veronica is a lifelong editor who left corporate America to found her own editing company, Write There With You LLC, to help aspiring authors bring to life the "books in their heads." She lives in Twinsburg, Ohio. Debbi, an accomplished vocalist, church choir director, and businesswoman, has lived permanently with the girls since February 19, 2009.

Printed in Great Britain
by Amazon